JOY-JITSU

THE ART OF LIVING A JOYFUL LIFE

JOY-JITSU

Editing: Enchanted Ink Publishing
Book Design and Typesetting: Enchanted Ink Publishing

ISBN: 978-1-7390542-3-6 (Hardcover)
ISBN: 978-1-7390542-0-5 (Paperback)
ISBN: 978-1-7390542-2-9 (E-book)
ISBN: 978-1-7390542-1-2 (Audiobook)

Thank you for your support of the authors' rights.

WWW.BUDOBROTHERS.COM

JOY-JITSU

THE ART OF LIVING A JOYFUL LIFE

BUDO BROTHERS
DAVID BADURINA
ERIK ALLAN
KYLE MAHADEO

DEDICATION

It is difficult to quantify the gift that Joy Jitsu has been in my life. It was 2021 when Erik and Kyle asked me to be front and center for this project. Truthfully, I was in a rough state. Writing wasn't coming easy, and that negative voice was too loud and too clear. I recognized that the universe offered me a gift, and I accepted.

Fast forward, and I've developed a deep, meaningful bond with two of the most incredible people I've ever had the honor of calling friends. Erik and Kyle put their faith in my ability, and I did my best to amplify their message through this work. They have my deepest gratitude for this unforgettable journey as well as their confidence and faith in me.

I'd like to thank my boys, Miro, Hartman, and Jefferson for always giving me a place to focus my heart. To my beautiful partner, Jaclynn, thank you for loving, understanding, and grounding me when I'm lost.

And to any of you dreaming and aspiring to accomplish your goals in the face of your own challenges and adversity, I believe in you. You are a gift. The world needs you and your voice. Focus on gratitude, blaze your trail, and be great!

We are all Budo Brothers!

-David

DEDICATION

I would like to dedicate Joy Jitsu to each and every one of you who's supported and encouraged us along the way. This book would have just been another silly idea that we would've tried and given up on if we didn't receive your continual encouragement and support.

Thank you to my family who's been there for me no matter what. No matter how dark life can get, it's my family that has always helped me get back on track.

We are truly blessed. We are lucky enough to be living our purpose, being creative, being of service, and becoming our best.

Joy Jitsu is an art. The art of living a joyful life. And just like any art, you have to put in the work to get good at it.

I hope this book helps you tap into your true potential and gets you on your own path of self discovery. May this book help lead you to life full of joy. So no matter where you are in life, it's time to put on your white belt and begin your journey.

With gratitude,

-Erik

To my beloved wife Maria, my unwavering anchor, and to my extraordinary parents Allison and Russel, whose guidance and support have shaped me into who I am today. To my remarkable sister Krista and my brother-in-law Aaron, whose constant encouragement has been a source of strength. This book is dedicated to you for always empowering me to pursue my dreams with unwavering tenacity.

In my youth, I was labeled a slow reader and banished to the slow class in school. Never could I have fathomed that one day I would contribute to the creation of a book like *"Joy Jitsu."* I am immensely grateful to David Badurina for walking alongside us throughout this project and becoming a lifelong friend in the process. Thanks for helping give a single finger salute to all the teachers that did not believe in me.

Finally, a heartfelt thank you to my business partners Tiffany and Erik. Our journey is just beginning, and I am filled with anticipation to witness the indelible mark we will leave on this world. Together, we shall embrace challenges and triumph over them, shaping a future that reflects our shared vision.

May the pages of "Joy Jitsu" serve as a reminder to never underestimate the power of one's inner circle. They are the steadfast compass, guiding us as we navigate the vast ocean of life.

-Kyle

CONTENTS

FOREWORD

Sifu Harinder Singh Sabharwal
*Martial Artist, Philosopher, Author, Speaker,
& High-Performance Coach
Founder of Master Your Center and Jeet Kune
Do Athletic Association*

In a world that often feels chaotic and overwhelming, the search for joy can seem like a distant dream. Yet, joy is not a fleeting emotion or the absence of struggle; rather it is a way of being, a choice made in the midst of life's challenges. This is the essence of "Joy-Jitsu."

To understand "Joy-Jitsu," one must first grasp the meaning of its two core elements: *Joy* and *Jitsu*. Joy is not mere happiness—an emotion that comes and goes—but a deep, abiding sense of contentment and purpose that can be cultivated and sustained. *Jitsu*—a term often associated with martial arts, skill, or mastery —here signifies the disciplined practice, the way, of living a joyful life. Together, *Joy-Jitsu* is the art and practice of living with intentional joy, regardless of the circumstances.

The Budo Brothers, Erik Allan and Kyle Mahadeo, are your perfect guides on this journey. From the moment I encountered their brand, I was struck not just by their innovative products but by the energy and essence behind them. There is a spirit that animates everything they do—a spirit of perseverance, authenticity, and an unwavering commitment to making the world a better place. I am blessed to know them personally and know they will inspire you as they have inspired me.

In a time when many are stressed, overwhelmed, and disconnected from hope, the Budo Brothers offer a beacon of light. They have cultivated themselves through both triumph and adversity, and their dedication to the practice of Joy-Jitsu is evident in every aspect of their lives. This book is more than a guide; it is a map to a way of life that is deeply needed in today's world.

"Joy-Jitsu: The Art of Living a Joyful Life" is built upon eight fundamental laws: Perseverance, Gratitude, Authenticity, Purpose, Growth, Balance, Creativity, and Service. These laws are not just abstract concepts; they are practical tools for navigating the complexities of life. The Budo Brothers present them in a way that is both accessible and profound, offering readers a 3-dimensional approach to self-discovery and personal growth.

Learning is not a linear process; it is spherical, ever-expanding, and deeply interconnected. As you engage with this book, you will find that you can start anywhere and still be led on a transformative journey. Masterfully narrated by David Badurina, the stories and practical advice contained within these pages will inspire you, challenge you, and ultimately lead you to the realization that the journey itself is the reward.

Join the Joy-Jitsu movement and begin your own path to becoming a black belt in life. I hold black belts in many arts, but I believe the greatest art to master is that of Joy. Let the Budo Brothers be your Senseis on this path, guiding you toward a life of purpose, fulfillment, and, above all, Joy.

UNDERSTANDING
THE PRACTICE OF JOY-JITSU

Hi. I'm David.

About five years ago, through some random hunting online for martial arts content, I came across a company called Budo Brothers.

I saw two passionate guys running a company and selling something called a "Hood-Gi," and my curiosity piqued as to who was behind this idea. At the time, I had been running my own martial arts dojo for about eight years. I had a few hundred students through the doors weekly, and I had started a podcast called *In Here, We Earn*. My philosophy, which drove my dojo and the podcast, was one of accountability, responsibility, and being proud of where your hard work and dedication takes you.

It didn't take long before I realized that the two men behind Budo Brothers were on a very similar wavelength, so I asked to interview them. They accepted, and we had an awesome time doing a podcast episode together.

I didn't know it at the time, but that was my first step into the world of Joy-Jitsu. This was the concept of resonance, which we'll be touching on when we dive into gratitude and authenticity. Fast-forward a few years, and we went from this little feeling of synergy to launching the *Budo Brothers Podcast* together, and in spite of having been previously separated by 2,500 miles, we were sitting around a campfire surrounded by the incredible Canadian Rocky Mountains, exploring the theory of Joy-Jitsu as friends together in order to prepare for the book you are holding in your hands right now.

These pages are a manifestation of the kind of incredible things that can happen when you accept the direction the universe takes you.

USING THIS BOOK

Like any journey, it helps to have a roadmap that allows you to see where you are and where you are going. A lot of our conversations in this book will be centered around metaphorical language. Erik, Kyle, and I tend to communicate through analogy, and this book is written through that lens.

This isn't a textbook or a straight-up reference manual. Joy-Jitsu is a practice in real life, and the best way to teach it is through examples and experiences, both real and abstract. This best allows you to shape and mold these concepts to your life. This is your path.

We break Joy-Jitsu down into the following concepts:

- Perseverance
- Gratitude
- Authenticity
- Purpose

- Growth
- Balance
- Creativity
- Service

Each of these concepts has a dependency on the one before it, and all of them connect and intertwine to form the full picture of Joy-Jitsu. We recommend your first trip through this book be from start to finish to complete that full picture. Once you've walked the path, use this book as your own personal beacon to reference when you're feeling a little lost.

At the beginning of each section, we are going to embrace a metaphorical journey from a dark and unknown place to a place of confident joy. Step by step, we'll use this metaphor with each section to help visualize the path you're setting out on.

Setting the Stage

I can best explain the journey of Joy-Jitsu by asking you to picture yourself lost and alone in the woods. It's dark, cold, lonely, and dirty. You have no map, no sense of direction, and are surrounded by the unfamiliar. Every sound—trees creaking in the breeze or a distant creature scurrying through rustling leaves—raises your anxiety. Your head is on a swivel, and safety is nowhere to be found. All you have are the clothes on your back and a single match. The only thing you can depend on is yourself. Happiness is in short supply.

This is where we begin our metaphorical journey into Joy-Jitsu.

In reality, we know that as time goes on, life becomes more complicated. All kinds of circumstances—some within your control and some a direct result of mistakes—have put you in a troublesome place. This is your own personal version of being lost in the dark woods. Maybe finances and relationships have been unsteady, or perhaps you've made mistakes in your career and business. Whatever these contributing factors are, each trial you endure makes every day more difficult.

Yes, this situation sucks. Life can be hard and comes with a great deal of pain. We all have our flaws and errors to account for on top of it all.

But you have a tool in your hand that will help you through this. By the end of this book, you'll be walking away from these dark woods with the sun on your face and clean air in your lungs.

Let's get started.

Your Journey Through the Dark—Light the Way

Our first goal on this journey is understanding how perseverance is an element of joy. The theme of this section is embracing acceptance and rejecting denial—to sit in the dark, cold woods.

Our first goal toward survival is to acknowledge where we are. Yes, it sucks being stuck in the dark. Nobody wants to be cold and alone, with no sense of direction. We don't want to be here because it makes us uncomfortable. Instead of frantically screaming or running as fast as we can without any idea of where we are headed, we accept and own the moment. That acceptance of our adverse situation is what can settle us. It's saying, "Okay. I'm here, and I am lost. Panicking gets me nowhere. Giving up gets me nowhere. How do I help myself right now?"

When you are afraid, panicked, or angry, you cannot see solutions. By relaxing, taking a deep breath, and understanding what perseverance is as a human living the human experience, you create conditions where you can move forward.

Acceptance won't solve our problems, but it is like striking a match in the dark. Think of perseverance as that match. It is the slightest flame that allows you to light the way. It lets you see reality more clearly. You are still damp, cold, and lost, but you can see. Radical acceptance of your circumstance is nurturing that tiniest flame to ensure it doesn't go out.

You may not realize it yet, but that little light is going to save you from hopelessness. It will allow you to see your surroundings objectively so you can find your way.

Now, let's light that match!

Our Natural State Is Joy!

When was the last time you felt joy? I'm not talking about a good day or a fun night out. I mean "felt joy" as in an overwhelming feeling of light and happiness where all of the daily crap you encounter was missing from your mind and you were fully in a perfect present moment?

The truth is, it is rare. The older we get and the more responsibilities shoveled onto our plate, the more rare pure joy becomes. You may have a great day at the zoo with the kids, but in the back of your mind, you're thinking about having to make the car payment as soon as you get home. Or that it's going to be tight shopping for groceries this week. Perhaps something happened at work, and while your little ones are laughing and marveling at an adorable otter floating around in a tank and looking cute as hell, you have an overwhelming sense of dread about work on Monday morning.

You could be out with friends on a Friday night, enjoying a cold beer and some conversation, but deep down, your heart is broken for any number of reasons. You're stressed out because you see people succeeding and you can't manage to get your shit together. Life feels like it is moving too fast, and those roses you're supposed to stop and smell once in a while are speeding by in a blur. You know that if you stop to enjoy a moment, everything is going to pass you by and you'll be that much further back from where you started.

As humans, we are not wired to live thinking only about grinding until the day we die. These lies we tell ourselves are both toxic and detrimental to our health and the health of those around us. All of this brings to the surface a question that needs answering:

What is our natural state?

If everything we build our lives around eventually turns into stress, why do we continue to subject ourselves to it? It's because underneath all the garbage foisted upon us day in and day out, we have buried a fundamental fact about ourselves as human beings: we are hardwired to persevere, and we are hardwired to feel joy.

When Erik, Kyle, and I were discussing this very topic, Kyle expanded on the concept of being hardwired for joy:

"Joy is like an internal light. When you are first born, there's nothing to dampen it. It's shining. You can feel it! If you hold a baby, that baby can light up a room with a smile. Babies emanate joy and love because they receive love from their parents, reflecting it back. There is no barrier for joy. When a child starts giggling at something, it's impossible to not feel how pure that joy is.

"But then, as you grow, the light dampens when things cover it up, shelter that light, and hide it.

"Your internal joy can be extinguished if you don't protect it. If you let that fire go out, it's hard to start it again. If you keep that flame going, you can feed it and grow it with only a little effort. Getting too beat up or bogged down by life, it's very hard to revive that flame."

There is real wisdom here. Joy is an internal fire. It warms you. It feeds those around you. It helps you survive the coldest, darkest times. Always having joy in mind allows you to keep those embers aglow and to feed that fire when needed. When life throws depression at you, and that flame goes out, it is so very hard to start it up again, but doing so is critical for both your survival and to help those around you.

Keep that fire glowing, no matter how small. It may rain on your flame, and it may take work to feed that fire, but figuring out how to make your fire stay lit is our way to cultivate joy in our everyday life.

Erik expanded on this analogy into the next step. How do we fuel this flame of joy within ourselves?

What is your kindling, what are you burning, and what helps that fire grow again? How can you eventually use your light to light the way for others?

"The goal is for that flame to not extinguish. What is the fuel for your flame? Family and the people you care about? Is it being outside in nature? Creating something? What is your therapy?"

I think we can learn by picturing joy as your own internal campfire and inner light. It allows you to see the world for what it is instead of fumbling around in the dark.

Your goal right now is to never, ever let that fire go out. Find the fuel for your joy. Protect that fire from the wind and the storms and the everyday trials and tribulations that do nothing but shovel dirt on your inner flame in order to extinguish it.

This is the first step of Joy-Jitsu self-defense.

Don't be afraid of the dark—darkness happens—but always focus on keeping that light going no matter how small, and you'll be surprised at how easy it is to reignite your own happiness into a raging bonfire that keeps you shining brightly.

When we had an opportunity to sit down as a trio and discuss this topic, I asked Kyle to tell me a story about a time where he felt his flame go out, and joy had disappeared.

If you're ever wondering how to find the things that bring you joy, perhaps Kyle's concept of *beacons* is exactly the touchstone you need:

"I always wanted to be an entrepreneur. When I was in Trinidad, I'd climb my grandpa's mango tree, rip all the mangoes down, set up a mango stand, and I'd try to sell the mangos. Little did I know everyone had a mango tree, but whatever; it made no sense, but that energy was inside of me. It was always to do something that would influence a lot of people or help a lot of people and be bigger than myself.

"So I started a gym. Fitness has been my life, and I've played every sport. I got a degree in kinesiology, and that was the perfect place to start a business because I understood the industry. I started by handing out flyers and got a couple of people to come to a boot camp. I worked my way up and eventually had a studio space where I had ten trainers and hundreds of clients. It was a business I was very proud of.

"The energy was great, the people loved the product, and I was very proud of it. But my business model didn't match my income. I ended up in a space that was too expensive to rent, and I always felt like I was drowning. No matter what I did on a sales front, it wasn't enough to pay for the rent. Then rent went up, and I had to get rid of the gym.

"When your identity is so tied to being an entrepreneur, and in your child's mind you're thinking you are going to be this rich and successful entrepreneur and retired by thirty, and you literally just get shot down, it's hard.

"I remember sitting at a gas pump one day, and I couldn't afford to put gas in my tank. I didn't know what to do. I had to call my mom to wire transfer me money for gas, and I just thought, 'Well, this sucks.'

"I talked to bankruptcy lawyers. I had no idea what was going to happen, if I was going to sell the gym or fold. I managed to sell everything for parts, get rid of it and offload it, but the amount of emotional turmoil rocked me.

"I worked on that project for ten years, and I was back to zero with no cash in the bank.

"I was depressed. All of my joy was instantly ripped away from me. Nothing was making me happy. Everything was stressful. I couldn't pay attention to people. I was always stuck in my mind.

"So I thought, *No matter what, what do I need in order to be happy? Something unrelated to anybody else in this world.* Because I noticed when I lost the gym, nobody gave a shit. The clients didn't care. The trainers were just wanting to get paid. All of the people that were so close to me as I was building the place didn't care, and it really rattled me.

"I knew at that moment that I couldn't make my happiness reliant on something else. So I said, 'Deep down in my core, what are the basic things that I can continually work on and progress with, because growth makes me happy?' So I came up with these things I call beacons.

"No matter where I am in my life, I can work on one beacon at all times. So if I feel lost, I can do something toward one of these things.

"Health is one of my beacons. I can control my physical health. No matter what state I'm in, that can always improve. I can always take a walk or do some yoga. I can always do something active.

"Creation is another one. I can always invent, create, or do something to fuel my imagination.

"Education. I love to learn and grow and build.

"Wealth is one of my beacons, and it's not necessarily money. You can acquire things that make you feel more secure whether it's physical items, saving money rather than spending it, or being a smart consumer.

"Relationships are another beacon. Even if you have nobody in your life, you can go to a coffee shop and strike up a quick conversation with someone and work on relationships.

"I picked these beacons because no matter where I'm at, nothing can harm these things.

"So if I am feeling super down on a given day, I can pick up the phone and call family and work on my relationships. It turns the day into a win. Or you can have a great day where you do a little bit toward each of these five things."

To pull some wisdom from Kyle's perspective, what are your beacons? These are the little embers of your joyous fire that you can always throw a little firewood on to solidify yourself and those around you. This is the nature of perseverance from an internal perspective as opposed to an external one.

Adversity Is Your Path

Back in 2011, I had the crazy idea to attempt a Spartan Race. For many people like me, it's less about the time to complete the race and more about finishing. I put myself through an intense physical gauntlet to test my willpower and not quit.

I signed up for and ran a three-mile race at Fenway Park in Boston, MA. There were about twenty obstacles across the race, ranging from rope climbing to rowing five hundred meters in two minutes, and a host of climbing, leaping, and running up and down stairs with a fifty-pound sack of sand across your back. It was brutal; it was a blast, and I loved every moment. After crossing the finish line, I felt like I was flying.

I was hooked.

A few months later, during martial arts training (I was running my dojo, working during the day and teaching classes five nights a week), I ended up with a back injury. It was months of fighting sciatica, moments of excruciating pain and immobility interspersed with weeks of feeling like I was improving, only to be greeted with one setback after another.

Obstacles aren't just physical things in front of us. Obstacles are mental blocks as well. Depression, anxiety, stress—these are things standing in the way of being happy and living our lives to the fullest. Being broken physically is a huge open door for mental obstacles to creep into your everyday life, and that's exactly what I experienced.

I gained a great deal of weight. I couldn't train. I could barely run through martial arts classes and leaned on some amazing assistant instructors to keep everything moving. Eventually, after months of failed rehabilitation, I had surgery to fix the issue. I had a disc that split in my lower spine and ended up crushing my sciatic nerve. The surgery was twenty minutes long, and the recovery took a few months. By mid-spring, I was feeling pretty good, though not up to the physical condition that I'd been in before the injury.

So I immediately signed up for three more Spartan Races. A Sprint (three miles), a Super in the ski mountains up past Montreal, Canada (nine miles), and finally the Beast in Killington, Vermont—a grueling fourteen-mile race up and down a massive ski mountain late in the year.

I wanted to embrace all the obstacles I could. I didn't care about my times. My only goal was to cross the finish line.

I completed the Sprint in New York and the Super in Montreal, and then on the Beast—seven miles into a fourteen-mile race—I slipped during a rope climb and shattered the bones in my left ring finger.

I had a choice.

Nobody would've batted an eye if I said, "Well, I tried, but the obstacles were too much." It was true. The mountain was menacing, the weather was driving rain and cold, it was getting dark, and I was running through the woods on the side of a ski slope with a fifty-pound sack of sand on my neck right before the rope climb. At seven miles, I was already exhausted and cramping. Then came the rope.

I knew immediately that something went wrong, and not just because half of my finger was pointing in a direction that should be physically impossible. I ducked into the medical tent, which was fortunately close to the rope obstacle, found some tape, wrapped up the finger, and promptly got back out into the cold and started running again.

Who wouldn't think about quitting at this point? It may have been the smarter choice, to be perfectly honest. But I persevered because there was something in my head that wouldn't leave. It was an emotion, a feeling, and a narrative.

"This is amazing. You are alive and injured, but you are going to finish this race. Cross that finish line!"

A few minutes later, I was on a net climb next to an absolute beast of a human being. This dude was huge, incredibly fit, and part of a CrossFit team. He had an insane amount of physical gifts yet was complaining about wanting to quit.

"Why do you want to quit?" I asked.

"Because this sucks. I don't need to abuse myself for a medal."

Sure enough, after we descended the net climb, he walked off toward the parking lot. My hastily taped finger, cramped calves, and burning lungs continued on. It was at that moment that I realized what understanding obstacles is all about.

Obstacles are the point.

In my mind, being injured, recently recovered from a back surgery less than a year prior, and being in worse physical condition than many of my fellow Spartans wasn't a reason to think I'm not good enough. Instead, it was a reason to complete obstacles until I could collapse past a finish line.

What did I get for almost ten hours of struggling through cramps, broken bones, and complete physical exhaustion?

A medal, if you're looking at something purely material. But if you look beyond the material, I gained so much more. I gained a deep, meaningful understanding that I have the capacity within my head and heart to persevere where others who are clearly more capable could not. This experience ended up being one of the most formative of my life. I paid about $150 to enter that race. I had to stay in a hotel the night before, there were months of training, and I was less than a year out from back surgery.

It didn't matter.

This is what obstacles can teach us. They are measuring sticks in every way. If that race were flat with no obstacles on a bright sunny day, it would have been a walk in the park. Its worth to my self-confidence was in direct correlation with how difficult it was, and even more so considering my injury halfway through.

Right after the race, caked in mud, I grabbed a bite to eat on my way to the ER, where the X-ray technician looked at an image of my shattered finger and only said, "David. What the hell did you do?"

When discussing this with my friends, Erik explained "adversity is your path" like this:

You can't get a benefit without experiencing the hardship that is tempering you. It is what gets you to a point where you can receive a gift. It's often not going to make sense while you're going through these challenges, but once you get through them, the gift is on the other side.

Feeling hardship and negative emotions and these things that we—on the surface—don't want, often are a precursor to make it through and get that gift.

"It could be something you learned about yourself—knowing that if you can persevere, you earn the gift. Each challenge is like a fight. If you've never fought or sparred, you're going to get hit all the time. When you practice and go through the pain of getting hit, the gift on the other side is that you learn how to move and dodge, then counter.

"Going through the pain of battling life's challenges is easier when you realize it is a signal that you are about to receive a gift. This mindest shift helps you cultivate an attitude rooted in perseverance."

Spending hundreds of dollars and putting myself through physical training and abuse in order to earn a medal was not the point. The gift was not a medal. The gift was the knowledge that no matter how daunting the task may be—and believe me, staring up at an 1800-foot peak when you're at the bottom of it is daunting—I can overcome it. If I could finish that race with a taped-up finger, collapsing across the finish line in exhaustion, leaving others behind that had no reason to, why would I need to be worried or fearful of an obstacle that's not even close to being that intimidating?

Everything changed in overcoming those obstacles. I became more relaxed, more confident, and far less beholden to terrible mental states like imposter syndrome and anxiety.

This is what we have to keep in mind in terms of perseverance. You have obstacles in front of you daily. Like hardening steel, each challenge you face and overcome strengthens your armor. As a warrior of life, welcome opportunities to become stronger and grow.

Embrace the challenge. Embrace the obstacles. You can do it by putting one foot in front of the other. The universe throws obstacles at you because it knows you will survive, and it won't throw anything at you that you cannot overcome.

So, overcome.

Celebrate your success.

Receive the gifts meant for you!

Understand What Is Within Your Control

You may not be expecting a callback to third-century BCE Hellenistic philosophical movements in a book titled *Joy-Jitsu*, but here we are. You may know the word *stoicism* as a philosophy, and you likely have heard someone referred to as *stoic*.

Let's start with a definition:

Stoic, n.—A person who can endure pain or hardship without showing feelings or complaining.

Stoicism was a philosophy brought to light in the ancient Greek and Roman worlds two thousand years ago. When you dive into this philosophy, you see names like Socrates, Epictetus, and Marcus Aurelius. In the modern day, there has been a definite renaissance of stoic thought, and it's because right now, we are all trying to persevere.

Hardship happens, and part of being human and living the human experience is understanding that we need to persevere. What better tools are there to help you persevere than an ancient philosophy that has truly stood the test of time—helping countless people over generations to become the absolute best versions of themselves?

One of the core principles of this ancient theory is very simple:

You do not control what happens. You control how you respond to what happens.

They referred to this principle as "the dichotomy of control," and it is a critical step in framing circumstances in terms that you can truly deal with. When I first got a handle on recognizing what events were inside and outside of my control, it was one of the most freeing experiences I've ever had. Internal anger and rage at the smallest circumstances withered away, replaced by relaxed acceptance.

This is such a powerful tool that you can employ with very little practice. When you feel that temperature rising, when something hasn't gone your way, this simple-to-understand ancient concept in stoicism is the voice of reason. It says, "There is nothing you could have done, but what can you do right now?"

We have a tendency when things don't go our way to blame external things. I didn't get a promotion. It was their fault. That chicken sandwich caused me to gain weight. Mother Nature was to blame for my being late for work. It was the man! It was a secret cabal of global influencers! We can go on and on finding external reasons for our failings, shortcomings, or adverse circumstances, but all of that wasted energy will not get you crawling out of the hole you're in.

A deep breath and understanding that the situation is what it is and the only focus that deserves your attention is the focus of getting out of it—now that's where the actual progress takes place.

A few weeks ago, Kyle and I were sitting in a coffee shop in downtown Calgary, and I asked him about his philosophy when it feels like everything's being piled on and it's so hard to shake it off:

"No matter the outside influence, no matter what is crashing down, no matter what battle you are in, the only thing that you can liberate yourself with is how you respond to those situations. It is the only piece you control. If you know and understand that, it sets you free.

"Think of all the words you use in daily language. Words like *I wish* or *imagine if* or *I would love it if . . .* But the only thing you can control is the present moment and your reaction to the external stimulus."

While I'm no interviewer, I really wanted to press him on the negative consequences of allowing these things you cannot control to take over your frame of mind. I prompted him with a scenario.

Pretend you're having friends over for a party. You'll be grilling, there will be tunes, and a bunch of people are coming. You bought all the burgers, you stocked the cooler, there were drinks and snacks, and everything was set and ready to go. And then?

A downpour. Something completely out of your control will ruin everything. How can this affect you, and how can you get past it?

His answer didn't disappoint:

"I would view it like this: It's easy to get paralyzed when everything external creeps in. There are so many variables that it takes away any kind of action. It's like being in a fight and thinking about what is going to happen, which is a great way to get caught on the chin. You're not in the fight; you're outside of it and trying to think of too many variables all at once without realizing that you simply have to react.

"Humans are adaptable. You can be present and mindful, and that allows you to be adaptable. Once you let go of all the stories that you tell yourself about how everyone's going to be pissed, and you wanted to show them a great time, and Mother Nature wrecked it, you can handle it. We figure out where else to cook the food, we reschedule, or we have an epic party in the rain!"

Erik added:

"One thing we've cultivated over the years is acceptance. We accept it is as it is. There is nothing we can do to change the weather or control an outside circumstance. When you accept the is-ness of the moment it's grip over your thoughts and rent free stay in your head vanishes. If you can drop the story and view what is actually happening, not what you think is happening, opportunity arises.

"Imagine being stuck in traffic. You can sit there fuming in your car, completely helpless to do anything about the situation, or you can see an obvious opportunity. Accept that the traffic is as it is, turn on an audiobook, and make the conscious decision to enjoy that moment instead of being pissed off at your surroundings, placing yourself in a position where you can only feel anger over something completely outside your sphere of influence.

"Can we use these triggers to observe our minds and see when we are upset, then ask ourselves what is within our control? Most of the time, the answer is to respond. Honestly, if you can sit back and observe yourself and understand that you are angry at something you have no control over, that realization of being in a bad mood can help snap you out of it. Why are you choosing to be pissed off?

"Instead of being mad, observe the feeling. You stop being it, and you understand it. Now use that feeling as a trigger to switch your mindset and adapt. 'How can I be the best I can be, since I'm reacting to something I cannot control?' That response is your power, and it is all you have."

So how powerful can this simple realization be? It sets you up for what Erik and Kyle like to refer to as a "No-Lose Situation."

Fighting yourself over something that you cannot control hinders you from action. It is, as Kyle described previously, paralyzing you. Once you make a conscious decision to focus on how you respond, you become free of that paralysis.

We know that the best lessons come through failure. When you go into a problem knowing you will either succeed or you'll achieve a lesson to become better in the future, there is no true loss. You understand that adverse circumstances happen, and you will either overcome them or learn how to overcome them with more expertise the next time they happen (and they will).

Never Fear Failure

There's something you should know about me.

I am a failure.

I have failed at everything I've ever tried. In fact, if you can picture for a moment a large cemetery—with gravestones as far as the eye can see—that is the history of my trial and error. It is an expansive field of memories that litter my background with blemishes, marks, bruises, tears, and blood.

Failed at relationships. Failed in business. Failed at work. Failed at games. Failed as a father, a son. Failed at passions, school, and friendships.

If we're going to put this on a truly accurate scale, I should also openly admit that one morning in 1997 when I was particularly tired and possibly quite hungover, I stepped into the shower with my underwear still on.

Yes, dear friends, I have failed at taking a shower.

As a child, I also stabbed myself in the eye with

my fork when I was eating. So add "failed at eating" to the list.

Ridiculousness aside, none of this matters. Why? Because failure is a weapon. In fact, failure may be the most ugly, rusty, sharp-as-fuck Sword of Eternal Power and Ultimate Victory you could possibly wrap your little failure fingers around. It's not some gleaming, polished blade, oh no. It's the most bloodstained, chipped, scored, and twisted hunk of scalpel-sharp steel you could possibly fathom. Whenever you take that beast out of its sheath, you know it's going to carve you up too, but there's nothing you'd rather have at your side when lost in the weeds.

When you've made mistakes and failed, it is much like being lost in the woods. You've strayed from the path, and now there is no path. There is nothing to light your way, and nobody to help you.

There is nothing but thorns and brush tearing you up with every step you take. And in the distance, you hear the howls of creatures waiting for you to stumble and fall again so they can continue to try tearing you down and tearing you apart. You've failed. They perceive you as weak—an easy meal.

That is, until you bring out that blade and begin carving through everything that stands in your way.

With every failure in your past, that weapon has grown stronger and sharper. It is forged from the honesty of looking at your past experiences. It is honed through every moment where you have tried something and failed spectacularly. Yes, it's ugly. Failure is not pretty. Yes, it's difficult to swing, just as your failures are difficult to handle. But it is yours!

Failure is a weapon of wisdom and experience, and once you realize that, there is nothing that weapon can't destroy.

And with each massive swing of that blade, obstacles fall. With each strike, it becomes easier to feel the weight and balance, and easier to wield. Before you know it, you are the virtuoso, taking your past experiences and failures and using them as a weapon to carve your way through the vines, thorns, and opportunistic creatures so intent on stopping you.

This is the mindset you achieve when you embrace failure and own it. It becomes more. It becomes an extension of you and yet another tool by your side to carve through the bullshit that stands between you and a step forward. Is it hard? Of course. It takes strength to wield that weapon. It takes pain and hurt and humility to learn from your failures and turn them into your power.

Thomas Edison said it well when questioned about all of his failures as an inventor: "I have not failed ten thousand times—I've successfully found ten thousand ways that will not work."

What about quitting? Quitting is comfortable, sweet, and attractive.

Quitting . . . is easy and comforting. Quitting is the simplest option when faced with the hard realization that you've made mistakes and you must now navigate through them. It's that little siren song in your ear that tells you the path is too difficult. The sword is too dull. You'll never cut through the brush.

Sit down in the thorns, because if you don't move, they won't cut you, right? There's no need to move forward. There's no need for the pain and scrapes and blood that it takes to push ahead.

Lay your head down. Don't try to progress. Let time slip by in silence. You're weary and tired. Haven't you fought long enough? Why subject yourself to more pain?

Quitting is that sultry voice that fills your head with alluring lies. "The way forward is too hard. You'll never be able to do it. There's only suffering that way. Turn back to where you were comfortable. Forget the unknown, because if you don't walk forward, at least you won't get hurt!"

In my time hanging out with Erik and Kyle, I've heard them both use the phrase "fail fast." Failing fast is the act of not dwelling on those missteps. You don't look around. You don't spend time listening to that voice telling you to quit. You fail. You accept. You do the work to extract wisdom from your circumstance. You draw your blade and cut your path forward.

This brings us to a concept that Erik and Kyle discuss frequently: No-Lose Situations.

Kyle describes it like this:

"We came up with this terminology because you can't lose when you make a decision. When you make a decision, you will either achieve the desired outcome, or you won't. Many people will take that failure of not getting the desired outcome and tell themselves they failed and lost. We know that the best lessons come through failure.

"You don't learn as much when you succeed. You learn the most through failure. When you go into a problem telling yourself you will either succeed or you will learn a lesson to make the path easier for the next time, there is no loss.

"This takes away the fear of trying."

When thinking about what it is like to fail, turn the word into an acronym.

First.
Action.
In.
Learning.

Learning from your failures and embracing them is what makes you capable of moving forward with success in your sights. Babies eventually walk even though they fail time and again trying. Humans redeem themselves after their errors and mistakes because we learn and adapt after our failures.

Whether it's a business folding and failing or something as simple as showering with your underwear on, you will learn!

Be Comfortable in Uncomfortable Situations

Let's try something together.

Close your eyes. Or, if you're in a social situation reading this and that would be weird just focus instead.

All I want you to think about is something you're going through that requires perseverance on your part. Take a moment to reflect on this troubling situation.

Maybe it's a relationship. Maybe it has something to do with work or training. Perhaps it's persevering through a tough time with a family member or a recent loss. Whatever it is that's down there, deep in your gut, affecting your happiness, put it into focus.

Go a step further. Hold out a hand and imagine you holding this situation. You can see it from every angle. The light is bright, all of the aspects of this situation—the complicated patterns, the painfully sharp edges—all perfectly clear and visible to you in the here and now.

It's hard. It's heavy. The sharp edges are cutting into your hand, and it's difficult to keep it held high as you analyze it, but you fight through that discomfort and study this manifested difficulty with the most discerning eye.

Now let's understand one simple fact about this situation:

You are designed to endure it.

This object in your hand—the manifestation of whatever difficulty it is that you're hanging on to, whether it's family, business, addiction, or depression—you are holding it up and shining the brightest light on it. Nobody is judging you. Nobody is staring at you. It is your own pain that you are confronting. Yes, it's stinging your palm, but you remain determined to keep this uncomfortable circumstance out of a dark, locked box.

Kyle shared his thoughts on this in terms of running a business:

"Once you are comfortable with adversity, it allows you to make the right decisions to propel yourself forward. Let's take it into the frame of entrepreneurship, because it is literally chaos and failure. That's all it is. Your ability to deal with chaos and failure and mold it in a way that allows you to progress. The faster you can understand that, the more you can settle in and persevere."

Perseverance is about enduring, and indeed you are designed to do so, but it is also about patience and honesty. Being patient with yourself knowing you are learning and figuring yourself out, and being honest with yourself in doing so.

Telling yourself lies to make the sting go away is like putting a glove on before holding that difficult circumstance in your hand. It's there, you see it, but are you truly confronting the uncomfortable circumstance? Are you truly internalizing the difficulty and pain that it's causing you? Are you uncomfortable, or are you fooling your own sensation?

Erik added, "Look at human history. Humans have endured endless wars. Plagues and disaster after disaster, and we're still here. You can do this!"

As a human being, we collect these difficulties, and we forget something very fundamental about the human experience.

We are animals, we are part of nature, and nature is ruthless.

I'd like to share a conversation we had about this very topic as it relates to embracing discomfort and looking to nature as inspiration:

Kyle: "Nature is hard-core. If you think about it, your job is perseverance and survival. The fact that we think everything should be easy and comfortable is completely outside of nature. When you are in nature, you have to survive. You have to find water and food. You have to persevere, or you're done."

Erik: "Eat or be eaten! Nature is raw. It will consume you. It doesn't give a fuck about your feelings.

Nature doesn't care about your feelings. Those laws apply to us. Who are we to think we are above the laws of nature?"

Kyle: "You know, fairy tales messed this up! Like, oh yeah, everything is magical, and we are owed happiness and all of these things. The reality is that nature is out to consume you. It's a jungle for real. If you go into the jungle and you aren't prepared to adapt to that environment, you're dead."

Erik: "We are living in a state—due to human ingenuity—where we have abundant energy and the creativity and means to solve huge problems. We have created a life that is incredibly easy. The problem with that is that we have it so easy in historical terms that we are now being challenged by ourselves. All of a sudden we are making up superficial challenges. Oh, nobody liked your selfie? That's the biggest worry? Really?

"Where this comes from is a place of ease. If you seek comfort, you will be met with challenge. If you seek challenge, you will be met with support.

"This is how the universe works. If you don't seek challenges, they will find you. If you go into the challenge having sought it, the universe has this amazing way of giving you what you need. The right person at the right time arrives. All of a sudden the universe is behind you and supporting you because you are actively going across the fire. You're scared, but you're going to walk across those hot coals even though every part of your being tells you not to."

Kyle: "And remember that everything has a cost. Hard work. It doesn't come naturally or organically. You want to get fit? You can't do that by watching YouTube videos. You have to put in the work. You want to be a millionaire? You have to give up things to achieve that lifestyle. Same with being a nun. One way or another, you'll have to pay."

Erik: "And to wrap this up, when we look to nature, the answer is there. If we challenge our muscles by lifting heavy things, we get stronger. If we put a cast on our arm, it atrophies. Sometimes we need the support! We broke our arm! It needs a cast! But if you don't take it off, you will have a toothpick for an arm. Nature will whittle you down if all you do is look for support.

"Face it. Life has a unique way of humbling you, and you can only truly move forward once it does."

One of my favorite things about my friends Erik and Kyle is that they have walked this walk. Life challenged two men that were dreaming of more. Instead of hiding, they embraced the difficulty and told themselves, "We are going to start a business. We are going to go to Asia to figure out how manufacturing works. We're going to pay the price to achieve what we want."

And they did.

They paid through sweat; they paid through mistakes, costly failures, and more. But just as you and I did at the very beginning of this particular chapter, they held that difficult circumstance in front of them. They studied it, they became comfortable with the pain, and they overcame.

And we will, too.

44

Your Journey through the Dark— Grow Your Flame

Negativity spreads. It is the cold rain from the night sky, soaking everything. It can take over our thoughts and mood. Negativity affects our relationships, feeds our ego, and prevents us from seeing clearly.

We've only just begun our journey out of the woods, but we have persevered and lit our match. We have accepted that we are lost, and now is the time to fight negativity and grow our flame.

Our next step is gratitude.

We have accepted that we've lost our way, and while we're far from finding our way out of the woods, hope is in our hands.

If perseverance is our match, gratitude is a handful of dry kindling. When you have endured, you are able to appreciate what is around you. Without gratitude, that match will go out. We are not built to only endure, after all. So we use that match to light a small fire that can survive a little wind and a little rain.

That's how perseverance and gratitude work together on our journey out of the woods. Life offers incredible experiences if you can see clearly enough to recognize them. With each thankful moment you recognize, your flame grows brighter and stronger.

Let's grow our flame!

Be Grateful for the Unwanted

In November of 2022, I was sitting in a living room with Erik and Kyle. We were talking about Joy-Jitsu and diving into this philosophy and sharing personal stories. When the topic came to gratitude, I asked them a straightforward question that has weighed heavy on my heart for a very long time:

"How do I train myself to be grateful for something that I don't want?"

Erik took the lead. "If we realize that whatever we're going through that's knocking us off our center and into a state of depression, there's a reason for it.

"Whatever is going on will not make sense until it's in the rearview because often our time of crisis is the foundation for future success. Once you've built that success based on whatever crisis it came out of, and you've made it to that beautiful point of achievement, you realize that you couldn't have done it without that challenge.

"Now you can say, 'Wow, I'm so glad I went

through that. I was at the bottom of the pool, unable to breathe, and now I'm here!' You know that if you hadn't gone through that, things may not have worked out.

"If you are grateful for the place of success that you are in, how can you not be grateful for that situation which led to the success? If we can be grateful for it, and we know that the challenges in our lives are here to serve us and help us level up, we can be grateful for it in the moment as well. That trial put us back on the path that destiny wants us on.

Gratitude snapped me out of the deepest depression of my life. So much so, that I became grateful that I went through that depression. If I can be thankful for that, then why can't I know that if something is going to serve me in the future, I can be grateful for it in the present. I know it's going to serve me in some way. It's going to open a door that was previously locked."

I remember hearing his answer and thinking, "Holy shit that's a paradox!"

Erik highlighting depression in particular hit my brain hard. You see, in February of 2019, I was two thousand miles away from home. My plane had just touched down in Las Vegas, and I had a funny text exchange with my big brother (who was perpetually fighting technology, often with humorous results):

He was fifty-four years old and healthy, and on the morning of February 8, he was scheduled for a

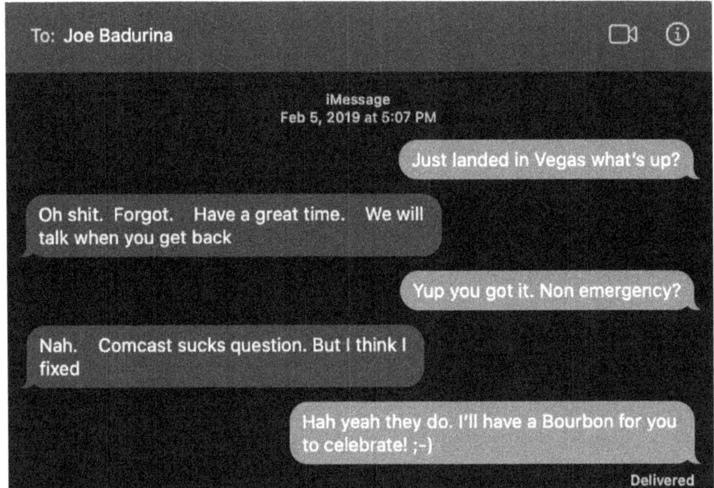

quick, routine shoulder surgery to clean up some scar tissue. When he was getting prepped in the hospital, surrounded by friends and his kids, he dished out some love and told everyone he'd be right back.

They wheeled him into the operating room.

Around noon on February 8, a little more than an hour after his scheduled surgery, I received a phone call. I was sitting at a restaurant on the Las Vegas Strip, waiting for a beer and a plate of nachos. It was my sister. I knew something was wrong as soon as I saw her name flash across the phone screen. Then came her words, escaping through choked tears.

"David . . . We lost Joe."

His fifteen-minute surgery caused his heart to fail as the anesthesia wore off. For an hour they tried time and time again to revive him, only for his heart to fail every time. Each time they thought they brought him back, his heart couldn't find the strength to keep going and he slipped away once more.

That was the end.

In a blink, my life was upside down. What was it like being in the party capital of the United States when you've just been informed that your big brother—your hero, your role model, someone who has been with you through some of the most difficult times you've ever had—was gone forever?

I couldn't handle it.

I don't remember much other than the waitress giving me a hug and handing me the packed food to eat later. The manager offered condolences and free nachos. I was on the phone with family and friends for much of that afternoon and evening. I remember forcing myself to eat soggy chips and cheese a couple of hours later.

Like most people on vacation in Las Vegas, I barely slept for the next few days, but not for the same reasons. I shuffled aimlessly around malls like a zombie and stared at happy, laughing people from this other side of reality where it was growing darker and darker. I was a distant, checked-out alien walking among humans I didn't understand. I felt like I was sinking into the ocean, and all of the sights and sounds and sensations that were so clear at the surface were quietly fading into silence as I descended into the deep.

On the flight home, I remember it being night and seeing the lights of Buffalo, New York, about thirty thousand feet below. I refused to listen to music because I didn't want to associate anything with the suffering I was going through. I remember wishing the plane would just nose-dive and smash into the ground, because I couldn't stand how much it hurt.

Depression made its grand entrance.

The notion—as Erik stated above—that I could be grateful for that depression would have been ridiculous had you told me at the time. My brother's death still ripples like a large stone thrown into a calm pond. There is still pain, still hurt, still fractures that will never be fully repaired. I remember that day when I eat nachos, as ridiculous as that sounds. I remain both eager and afraid to return to Las Vegas to forge new memories—it's a place I've always loved, and that negative association feels unfair. But this was the seminal dark moment of my life. Now, days arrive, and I feel productive and happy, but I know that at any point it can all crash into a fog of grief and tears.

And so, after a long break, I started writing. One of my last conversations on the phone with my brother was about the book I had just started, my first novel. He was excited for me and proud of me for starting something I've been wanting to do for years, and he wanted to hear more about it when I got back from my vacation. But those fractures—they ran deeper than I could've thought. Depression sank in its teeth and took over. The book stalled, my marriage failed, and a year later came the news that my father had a terminal cancer diagnosis and had about three months to live.

When it rains, it pours.

These were not events I felt I could be grateful for. But what if I—as Erik suggested—look at where I am now? What if I focus on gratitude and try to grow that flame, even just a little?

I wrote through the pain and finished that novel, pouring my heart and my pain into those pages and that story, and it has resonated with readers across the world. I have people messaging me telling me that they read my book for comfort in their own lives, and even if it is just fiction, it impacts something deep inside. Strangers tell me about the chapters they read that made them cry. I receive emails and reviews from people who tell me my book is what got them reading again, in some cases after many, many years.

That lost chance I had to speak with my brother one final time changed into a determination that I would be beside my father as he left this world, and I was. For two weeks he held on without speaking a word or opening his eyes. Every day as the cancer was taking him, his breathing quickened, and the rattle in his lungs got louder. I sat beside him every moment I could for weeks, holding his hand. When the moment came, and his eyes opened with his last breath, my voice was in his ears.

"I love you, Dad. We are going to be okay. You can let go."

I am not grateful that my brother and my father are gone. But if not for my brother being that crazy, beautiful hero who always wanted me to have success, I'd have not finished that book. That loss, and that depression, fueled me. And were it not for that loss and the crippling pain of being two thousand miles away from home when it happened, I may not have had the absolute honor of being a son comforting the father who held me as a child.

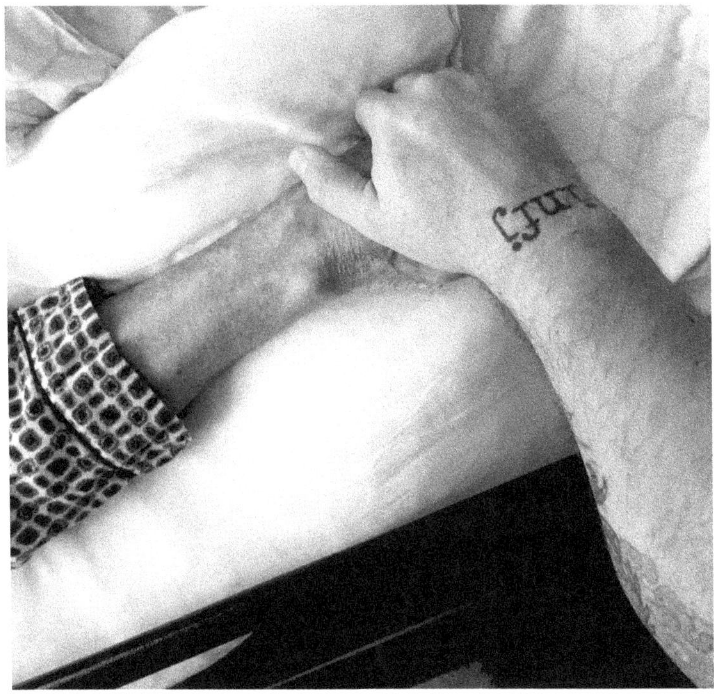

You know, as humans, we remain so shortsighted in terms of our experiences. The lesson in my story, and in Erik's poignant thoughts on gratitude, is this:

Some of life's most tragic, difficult moments are the exact moments that shape you into something stronger. So breathe. Relax. Step back and see your difficult trials for the gifts that they are.

You are not soft because you cry. You are not weak because you break down. You are not pathetic because depression and sadness take over. You are a human being living the human experience, and the universe won't put anything in your hands that you can't handle.

You are strength.

Magnetic Positivity

Years ago, I worked in a now-defunct chain computer store called CompUSA. I spent five years at various locations, and like any other retail job, it could be a challenge.

Retail is a mess of different personalities. Any moment you can have a thrilled customer, an angry customer, or someone trying to steal something off the shelf because they don't value property or law. When I started, I was a cashier, and believe me, I ran into all kinds of people.

Angry customers I could handle. They'd complain, I'd sympathize with their concerns, but they rarely took anything out on me. I was always there to help, and I always wanted to do my best in doing so. Rude people were part of the landscape as well. They'd be irritated having to wait in line or at the price of something, not say "thank you" and roughly grab their bag of paid-for items, and storm out of the store. There was nothing I could do to help.

The people who were most confusing to me?

The positive people.

See, I'd always ask someone, "How are you today?" I'd never meant it as a platitude or something you just say instead of hello. I'd look them in the eye, and I wanted to know what their mood was and how their day was. At my heart, I'm a positive person, and I always approach people from a viewpoint of how I can help.

When I asked someone how they were doing, and they answered, "I'm doing great today!" Well, I'll be honest.

It confused the shit out of seventeen-year-old me.

They're not complaining about the weather, they're not wandering around a giant computer store confused, and they aren't upset at the prices or at not receiving help. They were just great?

Yes. These were people that were grateful. Grateful to be in the store. Grateful to check out the latest gadgets, and indeed grateful that someone asked them a genuine question with a mind to help them.

You see, positivity begets positivity. And there's no greater environment for gratitude than a little bit of positivity.

Years and years later, when I met Erik and Kyle, I had that similar feeling. At first, I was confused. Wait, life is hard. Business is really hard. How are these two dudes so damned happy to simply be putting in the work? But getting to know them and to know that mood, it was something I could easily identify:

These are two highly grateful people. Grateful for every moment. Grateful for every interaction. Grateful for each and every failure and obstacle. Grateful for every success. They remain positive and grateful because they want to attract positive and grateful people into their circle.

When we sat down together in the shadows of the Canadian Rockies, crisp cool air in our lungs and an amazing breakfast in our stomach, Kyle explained his thoughts on positivity and attraction:

"You want to pull good moments or get the moments to work in your favor and go your way.

"We know people who always bring darkness around them. They can never figure it out. They always have bad things happen to them. That's what they attract. When you are properly magnetic, good things happen."

He pointed at me.

"Look at you! Good things happened out of nowhere, and opportunities came because you were attracting them! We're doing cool things together, and you're sitting here in the mountains with us working on putting together a book because your gratitude and positivity for people and moments project farther than you could have possibly imagined a short time ago. And it worked both ways. We find ourselves in a great moment together working on something meaningful."

It was such a simple and obvious observation, and it goes back to our previous discussion about perseverance. You'll recall in that section, Kyle described his theory about beacons. These are the touchstones. The lights in the fog that show him the way when times are difficult.

What became clear to me when he described the moment we were in working on this book is that my magnetic positivity drew me to something. My experience being with two friends hanging out in the Canadian Rockies working on something deeply philosophical and impactful had become an unforgettable moment in my life.

I found one of my beacons.

Being given the opportunity to visit my friends in person—sitting down together, sharing great food, music, and laughter while working on something deeply important to each of us—has become an anchor for me. When I find myself struggling with how to form the words, I remember being back in that place. I focus, knowing that we are all working toward the same thing—being of service to others through our own experiences in perspective.

I think about the great music we shared with one another, the great meals we shared, and how we had gratitude for every moment working toward a common goal of progressing through this project. You are reading this book because the three of us have persevered through our own trials. We stayed positive. We focused on gratitude. As a result, our positivity drew us toward something bigger.

We'll approach some of these concepts in future

chapters, but all of this leads to what Joy-Jitsu is all about. Persevering, having gratitude, and being yourself.

But what if you find yourself to be that negative person? What if your magnetism is for darkness, sadness, and negativity?

Can you change it, much like a magnet being flipped to switch positive and negative poles?

Erik explained:

"You can change this so easily. When it's dark and you're in your own head and you're convincing yourself that the world is going to be over, find one tiny, simple thing you can be grateful for.

"'I'm grateful for this cup of tea.' Boom. An immediate energy shift from negativity to being thankful and grateful. If that can be the spark that changes your day, maybe you're going to be attracting more positivity as a result. Do something that you love. Connect with someone you care about. Go back to the basics that can elevate you.

"Take on a challenge. Try a new thing. All of these things are internal and positive—they attract more of the same. Pray! Meditate! Observe nature. Feel the air go into your lungs. When you are in the present moment, your positive energy increases. Work it into your daily routine. Smash water. Say an affirmation. Think about what you are grateful for.

"The best advice I can give is to try to reach a state when you start your day where you almost want to cry because of how grateful you are for the positive things around you. Do that, and your day is going to be great."

When you get your headspace into being positive, you go through your day radiating that magnetism. It won't be long before you find yourself pulling all of the great things toward you.

Family and Friends

When I was a five-year-old, my parents brought me to a family picnic. Now, when I say family picnic, I'm talking about a large extended family all getting together outside at a large public park in Astoria, New York. You see, my family is from Croatia—Yugoslavia back then—and when my parents came to the United States, like many immigrants, they settled in and around New York City.

I don't have a lot of memories about this day, but there's one memory in particular that sticks with me. There was a relative of mine (and I don't recall exactly who, other than the fact that his extraversion terrified me at the time), who was always messing with my parents. When I say "messing with," I mean pranking and generally being a bit of a troublemaker to get under my mother's skin because Mom can be pretty high strung.

So he called me over when my mom wasn't looking, and I reluctantly approached him. He told me not to worry, then smeared ketchup all over my face, slapped my backside, and sent me to my mom crying. So of course, I run to my mom screaming. She thinks I fell down or got my face caught in a woodchipper or somehow ended up with blood all over me and freaked out, much to the entertainment of my other relatives.

While this isn't a fabulous memory for yours truly, I can look back at it in hindsight and remember some very clear details.

First, I was terrified of the man because he was loud, laughing, and joyous nearly all the time. That memory is very, very vivid.

Second, I remember my mom's shocked face at her son covered in red goo and the feeling of napkins wiping it all off.

Third, I remember Mom, after realizing she was pranked, laughing and saying she was going to slap the shit out of him.

Lastly, I remember a lot of family, food, fun, tra-ditional Croatian songs being played, the outdoors, and the smell of hotdogs and hamburgers on the grill.

This was never a truly bad memory for me. It's just something that was (and I was so young that I don't remember more than these details, but they're firmly in the memory bank). I miss days like that, where there was extended family everywhere, animated discussions, and all of that laughter on a perfect sunny day in Queens.

I could look back at this and think, "How terribly that man treated me!" That's ridiculous, though. There was only love in that park on that day, and recalling it now offers me an opportunity to have a ton of gratitude that I was a kid surrounded by so much family and have all of the memories as a result.

This is what family can do for us. Kyle described family and family relationships as a beacon—a light in the fog showing him the way to navigate through the tough times as he perseveres, but family is also an endless source of gratitude.

There's another point about family, as Erik explains:

"Family is so important, and it doesn't have to be blood! Family are the people you truly care about that are deeply involved in your life. They are so critical to your mental well-being. They are foundational in your security and support. These are people that are a sounding board or just pick you up when you're down.

"Having relationships with people that you can trust one hundred percent allows you to be grateful for more things in life. It's this base layer, like, if things really go south, I can always move back in with my parents. I can always stay with a friend. Someone has my back. This is the safety net of lifelong relationships.

"Having that net allows you to go out and take risks and take on new challenges without having to kick yourself out of the game before you even start.

Family has a way of cutting through the bullshit of your own self-doubt. Those thoughts that sabotage you moving forward get dispelled by the people who are closest to you and know what you're really capable of.

"It's the support network. And not everyone's going to have great families—there are a lot of broken families out there, and it's something we can heal from so we can work on creating new relationships that become family."

Kyle took the idea of non-blood family and expanded on it:

"Family is the cornerstone, and you can build a family that is outside of your relatives. This has been the reason Erik and I have been able to build our success. Family is the support system that frees us to do the crazy things. It makes us not scared of failure. Community and family make things bigger than us.

"This isn't just about us; it's not a selfish thing. When you're in a family unit, you have a role in that family unit. It's your job to provide support to others as you are supported.

"The other thing family can provide is somewhere you can place trust. Even if it's not the outcome you desire—you may argue with family, but you can trust that your family has your best interest at heart. Even if I think my dad is wrong about something when I ask him for advice, his goal isn't to one-up me. It's not to trick me. It's because he loves me. It's love. Family is a source of love and trust, and if you have that, you can thrive."

I'm thinking back on this conversation, and I remember—much like the above picnic memory—thinking that family can be very fleeting. We don't know how long anyone is around for. One day the people closest to you can be gone—an imprint left in your head and your heart that remains unchanging as years go by, with no new memories added.

It's really hard when you lose those close to you, but if you take anything from these stories and these conversations with Erik and Kyle, it should be that family isn't necessarily just who you are related to. You have the capacity and capability to bring anyone into your circle by simply offering support and asking for support from those who matter and who remain close to you.

This is one step of the Joy-Jitsu journey. And personally, it has had me reaching out to people that I may have drifted from, because relationships matter. If I can be there for someone close to me, I know that people I trust will be there for me during my dark times.

I have a hunch you might be thinking about someone now—be it a blood relative or otherwise—that you appreciate and consider your close family. If, by chance, you've drifted out of touch as I have with mine, make the call.

Be grateful for those around you and grateful that you're strong enough to offer support in return. Erik, Kyle, and I are truly grateful that you are holding this book and going through this journey with us.

We are each in the Joy-Jitsu family, after all.

Your Journey Through the Dark— Becoming You

We found ourselves in the woods, we've persevered and lit the match, and we've started a small flame of gratitude.

Now, we do the work. Authenticity happens when we drop the mask, stop trying to please everyone, and accept ourselves. When we understand and embrace who we are without feeling like we need to apologize for it, we find our internal north. Authenticity lights up our path forward. It helps us to recognize which directions are wrong for us, and it helps us stay the course no matter the strength of the storms around us.

We have taken the first step in persevering, accepting the situations we find ourselves in. We have focused on gratitude to emanate that light from ourselves so our flame can be strong. Now, we stand firm in who we are and set that fire free.

Authenticity takes work and honesty. Like gathering logs in the woods to cultivate a campfire, authenticity needs patience and care. When you know who you are, your way lights up. You can stay warm and dry with your own fire as opposed to depending on the flames of those around you. The surroundings in what were once dark, damp woods become bright and clear.

Authenticity is what ensures our fire is fed and strong, and the darkness gives way to our light.

Resonance

When I was asked to help put this book together, Erik, Kyle, and I had known each other for the better part of four years. I was a customer of Budo Brothers, but we also worked together. They asked me to help with the technical aspects of starting a podcast, and I helped them launch the *Budo Brothers Podcast* and co-hosted the first twenty or so episodes together with them. We shared plenty of stories, thoughts, and perspectives about martial arts, mindset, and life in general.

During that time, I got to know both of them well, including their backgrounds, prior work they've done, and fun details like Canada having ketchup-flavored potato chips. We've had lengthy discussions about the superiority of American-made Corn Pops cereal as opposed to the Canadian version, which from what I've been told resembles chewing pumice and can cause grievous injury to the inside of one's mouth.

Part of Erik's background I was previously aware of was his education in engineering. This is a guy who understands physics, the scientific method, and the subject of this section.

Resonance.

So I'm going to let him take it away:

"Resonance is a beautiful physical phenomenon if you actually understand the principles behind it in terms of physics. It will blow your mind.

"Everything has a natural frequency. When you hit a spoon against a glass, the ring you hear is the natural frequency of that glass. The sound begins when it is disturbed and quickly dampens off to zero.

"If I had the exact same frequency as that glass and had it on a speaker, the glass would begin to vibrate and eventually shatter. It's the opera singer breaking glass by matching the frequency of the physical object. She is singing the frequency of the glass. Being the same note, it activates the molecules inside of that glass. Since the frequency is an input, not an output, it excites the molecules, so much that it will explode!

"If you look at the mathematical equation for resonance—something I learned in one of my engineering classes regarding acoustics and optics—when the natural frequency equals the input frequency, the equation goes to infinity.

"That's when it breaks.

"Resonance is so cool because when something

excites us in our soul, it activates something in us. When something is caustic and toxic and against your energy, there will be people out there who resonate with it. They're going to love misery. They're going to love the bullshit. They'll love all of the dark shit because that's where their natural frequency is.

"So when we can get in tune with what is resonating inside of us, it pulls us into infinity. Resonance is that beautiful thing that takes you out of places you are not supposed to be and puts you into places that you are. We all resonate at a frequency, and everyone's frequency is nuanced and different."

Kyle added to this abstract concept of resonance like so:

"Imagine you're on a street with a whole bunch of different nightclubs. Now, you love hip-hop music, but the first bar you walk into is a full-on screamo bar."

(Author's note: For aging Gen Xers like me, screamo can be defined as screaming emotional lyrics all about your feelings to music that resembles happy punk rock. It's an acquired taste. Personally, I haven't acquired it, though I do like some My Chemical Romance when I'm feeling in my bag. Anyway, moving on . . .)

"So everyone in there is rocking and doing their thing, but it's not for you; it's not in your soul. So you walk down the street and go into a bar where they're playing dubstep. Definitely not your vibe. Then all of a sudden you walk into a bar where they're blasting hip-hop, and it feels in a strange way like relief. Like you can finally be yourself.

"We've always viewed a lot of the things we do as a concept of "island life"—we envision that we're playing massive drums, drums on this great island, letting that energy vibrate outward. And when people hear it—and it's their music—they're attracted to it. They're vibing with us. Now we're resonating, and they can come join us on that island."

I think one of the important points about resonance is that it is already inside of you. You have this frequency, and a lot of times we pretend we don't.

Look, I can pretend to be all kinds of cool around my friends. I can say that I love the same music as they do or the same shows. They may be all about watching *The Walking Dead* or *Game of Thrones*, talking about the latest horrific end to a beloved character. And if that's not how I truly resonate, I can say all day long that I love the shows too, but when I go home, maybe I'm throwing on some lighthearted rom-com like *Sleepless in Seattle* because I just need to eat some chocolate and have a good cry.

When we listen to music we resonate with, it moves us. When we watch movies we resonate with, we remember the stories and emotions they have invoked.

Now how does this tie in to authenticity?

Resonance is intuition.

We know when something is off. We feel it deep in our gut, and when we're able to be honest with ourselves, we understand it as a red flag. Resonance is that vibration—our internal frequency—and when we encounter something that resonates with us, we feel it in our gut—everything makes sense.

Resonance is based in natural law. Everything—every object—has a natural frequency. When we hit that frequency in an authentic way, our resonance is truly infinite. We've hit on something so deeply in tune with who and what we are that there is no possible way to fight it. We ring together with our passions and with people who matter to us.

Pretend all you want that you hate pop music, but when you're in your car by yourself, and you start belting along with Ariana Grande when her voice rings out on your car stereo, that's you being you.

Not everyone or everything will ring at your frequency. Not everything will vibe with you on the deepest of levels. However, when you get to know yourself, and you are honest and authentic, you will feel it deep down. You can't play pretend, and you can try to deny it as hard as you can because it's "not cool." Remember this: living by someone else's frequency is never going to be as fulfilling as finding your own.

Be you. Listen to your frequency and don't be afraid or embarrassed by it. Being a pretender is denying yourself, and those around you who are in tune with their own frequency will sniff out that inauthenticity in a heartbeat.

So go ahead and grab a big bag of ketchup-flavored potato chips, crank up the Ariana Grande, and sing your authentic heart out! You are the vibe!

Stop Caring About What Others Think

Erik recently told me a story about his love of skateboarding, and I can't think of a better example of what happens to you when you care too much about what others perceive you as:

"When I was growing up, I fell in love with skateboarding. It brought me a lot of joy—this constant challenge to meet the objective of landing a trick. I loved that there was no limit to what you could do as a skater, because it was always being pushed to new heights. Someone would land something unthinkable, and a few years later that was the new standard.

"Once you achieved a level of mastery, you started creating more and inventing new things. It was this beautiful pursuit of something that was actually not achievable.

"As a kid, I was so obsessed and on my way to becoming amateur—something more than just a neighborhood skater. I was known as a top skater in junior high in my hometown. I was the cool kid, bringing ramps to the school. There'd be a huge crowd, and people were cheering, and I felt like a god. It became a huge part of my identity.

"Once high school came around, skateboarding became less cool—my friends had older brothers who were now the cool kids. When skateboarding became less cool, all of my friends quit. I still really loved it, but now I was doing it alone and almost hiding it. Before I knew it, I'd convinced myself that it was no longer cool.

"I aborted a true passion of mine for the sake of other people's opinions.

"That was one of the first big mistakes I made in conforming, and that conformity definitely dampened my flame because I was being someone I was not. I was not being myself, I had false idols, I was trying to be someone else, and I was wondering why I was less happy.

"I didn't have that same state of joy because one of the big things in my life that brought me joy was skateboarding.

"Luckily, martial arts was there too, and it was still considered cool and useful, so I kept up with that. It was great because I could at least sustain something that was bringing me joy apart from partying and getting into trouble.

"After I graduated and realized there was life after high school, I asked myself why I stopped doing something I love. Why did I do that? And I got back into it and it reignited the fire, and I felt absolutely amazing!

"Why did I leave something that brought me so much joy just for the sake of conformity? These are pressures that we all go through, but rekindling these old activities that bring us joy can reignite our flame."

If you are on social media at all, you understand at least partly why "what others think" has become huge business. Everything we engage in is for likes and clicks. People have begun determining their worth from views, of all things.

Not what we communicate.

Not what we achieve.

Not who we are as a person.

Not our deeply held principles and beliefs.

Not what we stand for, fight for, and would die for.

But... views. We have become slaves to arbitrary algorithms in a world that is not physical or real. "Who saw it" somehow supersedes "who I am."

Kyle puts this into its proper perspective:

"I lost a business. I hit the bottom. Now, I just say whatever the fuck I want.

"That was the hardest emotional moment I had. It was then that I realized that people are so busy with their own problems that they can't even consider anything else. So why am I trying to put all of the weight of others on my back when I'm trying to go achieve a goal?

"The best way to help people is to simply become who you are and put your oxygen mask on, then help others from that place. People don't want to be told what to do. They learn best from you being authentic, on purpose, and on your path.

"So I went through all of this, and I was like a donkey walking up a hill pulling this huge cart. I knew that when I got to the top of that hill, I'd be able to help other people. Along that journey, though, everyone is piling their personal sack of shit on the cart. The more I hold while I'm trying to achieve on my own, the slower I'm going to go.

"If I just discharge it, not carry their shit but talk to them openly and honestly and just be myself, I'm going to have a faster journey. Might it get awkward and uncomfortable? Sure. You can lose friends. You can lose people.

"But you free yourself.

"Everything has a cost. In order to be truly free and authentic, you have to give up the fact that some of the things you may do or say will piss people off. Might make them upset or cause a fight. When you give up those things and focus on your journey, you feel better internally. Then you just rely on resonance.

"The faster you can get to your authentic self, the more you can resonate outward to bring in the people that matter to you."

Running with this donkey analogy, imagine all of those people Kyle described not only shoveling shit onto your donkey cart but talking the whole time.

"You're not going to make it."

"You're going to fall down like I did."

"Why bother climbing?"

"You're just going to fail anyway."

The last thing you want to do is listen and internalize that kind of negativity and end up sitting down next to them, halfway up that hill, all because they didn't achieve and they told you that you won't either.

Why listen to that?

Do you. Get to the top of the hill and get up there your way.

Erik jumped in:

"Look, nobody cares. There's a great meme I saw that was a cartoon of a sad, slump-shouldered character sitting in obvious despair. The words above him read, 'Nobody cares.'

"In the very next panel, it had the same character with this huge smile, his arms raised high, and it still read, 'Nobody cares!'

"But that's the point, isn't it? Nobody gives a fuck! It's so freeing! So you can sit there all sad and burdened by nobody caring, or you can be liberated because guess what?

"Nobody gives a fuck! Go live your life! Go live the fullest version of yourself! Tap into who the fuck you are and go make your mark!"

Kyle continued:

"Everyone's scared to be naked. That's the way you were born. We created clothes and garments and this society where certain things can be shown and others can't. Like you can't show a nipple on television. We created coverings to keep us warm from the environment, sure, but we created a society where we effectively hide our natural selves.

"You were born a certain way. The most natural thing is always the best. If you can be comfortable being metaphorically naked in a room full of people, you have all of the power. If you're able to present your bare, basic self and be comfortable in your own skin, you are the most powerful person in the room. But that's not a natural thing mentally for people.

"I'm not even close to that myself, but it's something to strive toward. Being completely comfortable."

Now, let's not all set a new standard of walking around naked in public. Understand what it means to be vulnerable, though. When you are your unabashed self and fully accepting of who you are, something amazing happens.

Nobody can tear you down unless you consent to it.

Don't consent.

That, my friends, is the power of authenticity.

Kill Your Jealousy

Authenticity is one of my favorite topics to explore because it has been a struggle to varying degrees at nearly every turn of my life. Who am I, really? This is a huge fundamental question. This is some cosmic stuff! It explores the nature of your mind and your actions in concert with everyone and everything you perceive and interact with every day of your life.

And out of this amazing question comes a simple mantra that we can apply to our life: your journey is yours.

Erik ran with this question and described the same feeling I had, culminating in the phrase "kill your jealousy."

"There's nothing wrong with looking at another person's journey as an opportunity to learn what worked for them. They aren't you, but you can watch what they did—what strategies, tactics, and methods they used to achieve a certain outcome. That can be a beautiful source of inspiration.

"But as soon as you try to copy somebody?"

"It's not going to work, because it's not you.

"It's very important to work on this—when you see someone successful, or when you see someone who has amassed wealth or did something incredible, often the default emotion is jealousy. You say things like, "Are you kidding me?" or "He's an idiot!"

"You are sending the wrong energy to achievement, success, and abundance. Try instead to be in admiration of other people's achievements. Tell them they're doing amazing! Good job! You're killing it! How did you do that?

"The trick is to become a seeker. Get involved in learning from them, because you can learn something you can take and apply to your journey. Seek how they did something. Basically, take a source of inspiration and go to your own lab and see if that chemical reaction can work. Does it react with something you can do? It's important to try to kill jealousy the moment you feel it and use that feeling as a reminder to switch to admiration.

"If you can admire that which initially made you jealous, you are so much more likely to put into action your own version of whatever lesson they were grateful enough to share with you.

"People are eager to talk about their successes. Ask questions! You'll get responses like, "Well, you're so interested, let me tell you about it!" Now you're providing that person value by validating their achievements and celebrating their success, but you are also learning from their tireless efforts, fuckups, and lessons that they had to grind through. You add it to your repertoire.

"It's a mindset shift to kill your jealousy and switch to admiration and curiosity. I had to work on that a lot. Especially when I was just in the pit. I was basically saying, energetically, "Some awesome shit is happening. Fuck that.""

"That is the wrong energy! You could call it luck or whatever, but they did something and got a great result!"

Let's talk about the zero-sum game.

In game theory, a zero-sum game is a situation where one person's victory is equivalent to another person's loss. This creates a net change in wealth of zero.

Think of it this way. If four people are sitting around a poker table, and they each have twenty-five dollars in their pocket for betting, the maximum any single person can take home would be one hundred dollars. Two people could each take fifty home, or one person can bring home ninety-nine, and another a single dollar. The other two would probably have some explaining to do to their significant others.

The beautiful thing about the zero-sum game is understanding that it does not apply to success or achievement.

Just because someone across the table from you brings home a hundred dollars does not mean you can't bring home a hundred, a thousand, or ten thousand dollars. Success is not a finite resource in any way. One person cannot hoard success just as one person cannot sustain all of the loss without any hope for gain.

Think of how beautiful and freeing that is. You can celebrate one person's incredible success and achieve a similar level of success on your own, and there's not a single thing standing in your way except for your actions. There's no finite resource to fight for, and you have the freedom and capability to simply be positive!

This is a circumstance I often saw in my dojo. People would keep their eyes to the side, staring at the higher rank that was beside them. Jealousy abounded.

"How did they get that rank?"

"My technique is better!"

"I should be that rank!"

Okay, congratulations. Go be that rank. Nobody and nothing is stopping you. Just because someone has a higher rank doesn't mean you have to sit there in the lower one. Achievement and success are most definitely not zero-sum.

In the writing community we see this as well, and it's maddening! Authors should be happy for other authors who see success. Instead, jealousy takes over, and people whisper about how someone else's success wasn't deserved or that their writing is trash.

Go on, then. Write better.

I had a particularly juvenile, triggered person on

YouTube comment on one of my videos in regard to my path to self-publishing my first novel. I merely showed a stack of positive reviews, and I was happy about it.

Their comment?

"Yeah, but you self-published."

That's what jealousy sounds like. Instead of "Congrats!" or "How did you do it?" there was a jealous dismissal. Nothing is stopping this person from publishing their own work, but instead of learning, they chose to be close-minded, jealous, and petty.

That will never lead to success. Just because I found a way doesn't stop anyone or anything from finding their own way. For the record, I'd have been happy to answer a genuine question about my process to help someone else as well. Open minds deserve open conversation. As an author, nothing makes me happier than helping other authors achieve success.

Think about how powerful it is to kill jealousy. You have no competitors, you can learn from anyone and anything, and you can find your own way. It won't belong to anyone else but you, and you can get to your success. That's some powerful stuff!

In martial arts, we're used to the title "sensei." We come to understand the definition as "teacher," but it's more than that. The exact translation is closer to "before life," though in the West we typically understand it to mean "one who has come before" or "those who have come before."

These are the experienced people that have found their way, made their mistakes, and walked their path. You learn from those mistakes and apply them to your own path.

Before we wrap up thoughts on killing our jealousy and embracing our authenticity, I want to touch on one great warning that Erik summed up like so:

"The one thing I'd add to finding your authenticity is to remember that it's exhausting to fake it. Drop the ego and don't bother trying to fool anyone. It takes so much effort to convince other people of what you want them to think you are, when you know in your core you aren't.

"The irony is, if someone has to tell you they're awesome—shocker—they're not awesome. If they have to constantly remind you of how great they are, they're not great.

"Be great.

"Do awesome.

"Be amazing."

Kill your jealousy, my friends. Let go and be authentically you.

Meditation and Reflection

Reflection helps you figure out who you are. You are not your thoughts. If we identify with our thoughts, and someone challenges our beliefs, we take personal offense because we are attached to them.

Meditation is a great way to detach and be the observer of those thoughts. We can watch them as if they are just clouds floating past. Like, "Hey that's an interesting thought... There it goes."

I believe the more you meditate the more you get in touch with your being, and that's where true authenticity lies. So, we can sit still.

I do it every morning in the shower, which is why I take long showers. I sit down, let the water hit my face, and meditate in the shower. It's impossible to be distracted, because I'm in the shower, and there's no phone, and it's a beautiful place to do it. I find it helps me get to that depth of who I am, which is almost beyond description.

It's an energy. An energetic entity that grows in the silent moments. Enhancing your awareness—what you are and what you aren't—it helps me figure out everything else.

Realize Your Power

I was sitting down with Kyle and Erik discussing this book and in particular this topic of authenticity, and we came around to the subject of "Realizing Your Power."

Kyle—without missing a beat—repeated this quote by Marianne Williamson, often mis-attributed to Nelson Mandela:

"Our deepest fear is not that we are inadequate. Our deepest fear is that we are powerful beyond measure. It is our light, not our darkness, that most frightens us. We ask ourselves, who am I to be brilliant, gorgeous, talented, and fabulous? Actually, who are you not to be? You are a child of God. Your playing small does not serve the world."

Power is an interesting topic, and this above quote is thought-provoking in that power can be scary. It's easy to be meek. It's easy to be afraid. It's easy to rely on flight every time the fight-or-flight response hits.

So I asked Kyle to expand on his thoughts on having personal power:

"If you really think about it, everything is attempting to steal our power. If you look at slavery—slaves were made to think that they had zero power. As a collective, they had no power whatsoever, but if they only realized that by moving in the same direction, they'd have all of the power; things would change.

"In Thailand, they use a small pin knocked into the ground attached to a chain shackled to an elephant's foot. That elephant believed it was too weak to be free, and so it would stay in that spot even though it could easily walk away. It was conditioned to think that this pin prevented it from going anywhere.

"Your power is that internal light. It's within you. Everyone has a fear of using that light to its full potential. We all have that immense power. You are afraid of action. You are afraid of being exposed. There are all of these fears surrounding your own power. It's like we're scared to be seen! We play small for people, and we don't go to our full potential.

"We know we are capable of doing anything. We have all of this capability to accomplish anything, but for whatever reasons, we play small. The power exists. It's just how do you represent it without being scared? We are the elephants trapped by a little pin, and that pin is fear.

"It's a fear of both failure and success. Maybe you don't think you're good enough, so you're not going to try."

I'll interject here to say that talking with Kyle is often like talking with a wise sage who also likes to curse and laugh. And when we have these types of discussions, I always come away with some kind of realization.

My realization here, and I'm hoping your realization as well: What is that pin made out of?

Here you are. Big, powerful, all the capability in the world, but something in you is afraid. Afraid of success or afraid of failure. What is it, and why?

Maybe you're afraid of success because success by its very nature changes things. Success is born from some risk. Success means hard work. Success is the late nights, the struggling, the fighting, and the creation of opportunity through sweat and tears that you wouldn't have if you took the easy way and sat your butt on the sofa with some snack food, mindlessly scrolling the internet and wondering why everyone else is having the success you aren't.

Maybe you're afraid of the failure. You have doubts deep in your heart, and though you want to try, and you want to spread your wings and soar—what if you fall? Nobody wants to have their own self-doubt proven correct, so it's easier to simply sit on the sofa with a bag of snack food, mindlessly scrolling the internet and telling yourself lies about how everyone is lucky except for you.

These are some harsh truths, dear reader. These harsh truths aren't meant to knock you down; they're meant to wake you up. You are that powerful beast, tethered in place by the most insignificant chain from which you can break free at a moment of your choosing, but you don't.

Why?

Kyle continued:

"We may be scared of being too successful, so we try to control the success we have. It's too good to be true, so we dial ourselves down and hold ourselves back. We can't possibly be this awesome and have all of the abundance that comes with it. It's self-imposed pressure and problems to dampen our own velocity of success."

This is something that we, as humans, do to ourselves over and over. We are afraid to jump in and take the plunge. We tell ourselves lies.

"I just got lucky."

"I guess I was in the right place at the right time."

"Lightning in a bottle."

"It'll never happen again."

Each one of these ridiculous sentiments is akin to us staring down at that pin in the ground and thinking we'll never be free. We ignore and dismiss the reasons opportunity came to us and success was achieved. We don't attribute it to the hard work we've done or the conditions we've created in order to see and seize that moment in order to have that success.

When Erik and Kyle started Budo Brothers, they had some ideas in their heads, a little cash in their pocket. And with those two things, and open minds, they walked forward and pulled the pin out from the ground. The success my friends are having today is a direct result of the action and belief they harnessed when nothing was holding them back. An outsider may look at Budo Brothers and the success Erik and Kyle have enjoyed and think, "Well, they got lucky and sold some products," or "Well, they knew the right people."

That's jealousy talking, of course. The fact is they created their success by straight-up ignoring the shit that was tethering them into the ground.

And both Erik and Kyle—today—may look at what they are doing in terms of the direction of Budo Brothers and think, "We're not sure if we should take that step." These kinds of thoughts are normal and natural for everybody, but they come down to looking down at that pin in the ground chaining you to that one spot and, for whatever reason, being afraid to step forward. Why? Because success was built and attained, and now there is something at stake.

That's what fear does. You have to keep the success going! You can't have a failure! People have expectations!

This is a fast track to mediocrity and stagnation.

So any time you look down and feel that pin in the ground, I want you to do us all a favor. Rip it the hell up and carry the hell on.

Your life isn't meant to be that of a dreamer—waking up, wondering "what if," working yourself into old age, and leaving the world with the same sort of silence you felt while you were here. No, this world needs to look like an expanse of grass filled with muddy holes and footprints because we all realized our power, yanked our pins out of the ground, and trampled every doubt and fear on our way to being truly free, realizing the power we've held all along.

Your Journey Through the Dark— Knowing Why

Perseverance, gratitude, and authenticity have set the stage for the next part of our trek out of these dark woods.

Purpose.

Purpose is knowing who you are through honest and objective observation. If we are to make our way out of this forest, we're going to need that strong fire of authenticity to warm us and prepare us for the journey ahead.

Remember, though, this is a journey, not a destination. It's the process of finding who you are and that fulfillment you achieve when your passions align in service to yourself and others. It is a never-ending source of motivation and joy that can only be seen and traversed when we are clear-headed and honest with what our core desires.

We've endured a dark night. We've started a flame and have grown it into a robust fire. The light we've managed to harness through being authentic has now lit the way.

A path is revealed. We light a torch to see the way and begin walking forward.

Welcome to the journey that is purpose.

Passion + Service = Purpose

We often hear phrases like:
"You were born for this!"
"You have a gift!"
"This was meant to be!"

All of these types of phrases related to your purpose or your destiny are common in movies and television shows, and you may have heard them yourself doing something you truly love to do. People recognize when you are in your element. When we have a talent for something we enjoy, our natural joy radiates out, and it's easy for people to notice. We are that child again, fully immersed in what we are doing and enjoying every second of it. People who witness that understand that feeling and how difficult it is to capture, so they experience our unfettered joy simultaneously. It creates amazing moments!

But what is that "thing?" What is that fleeting talent or skill or passion that we have locked away that is positively aching to be released and take flight? Why is it so hard to find, recognize, and honor?

Do you remember those Magic Eye puzzles that were so prevalent in shopping malls back in the day? When you looked at it in passing, it seemed like a haze of colors and patterns, with nothing discernible going on. People would stare at them for a long time trying to make out what the image was. The strange thing about these particular optical illusions was that you could only see them clearly when you didn't focus on them! That's what purpose has always felt like to me. It's that abstract thing, and only when I'm not sitting here pondering my purpose in a regularly occurring fit of existential dread do I find that I'm living it.

It's truth.

As an author, I spend a large portion of my time suffering from imposter syndrome. I'll spend days rubbing my temples, worrying about arbitrary deadlines that don't matter. Things like "writer's block" or "inspiration-less doldrums" is front and center. Then I start writing, and the words pour out free and easy, and I think, "Well, there it is! There's the passion!"

We do this about all kinds of things in our life. If you're in the dojo, you're worrying about testing or ranking. You worry about your health. You wonder if you can pull off techniques that are sharper than someone else who you've been watching for a long time. But when you're in the flow, it comes easily and naturally.

It's a wicked little paradox. Your purpose is only in focus when you're not focusing on your purpose!

So as I sit here writing and transposing portions of my conversations with Erik and Kyle, I hear myself on audio getting straight to the point.

"I'm trying to figure this out. What does this mean to you?"

Kyle took the lead.

"Passion is what excites you. It's what gets you out of bed. It's this feeling that you have. In order to find it, you've got to fuck around and find out! You have to sample a whole bunch of different things. Some people can do it in their youth; some wait until adulthood.

"You have to be settled. I do think that meditation and things such as slowing down help you to observe your actions and reactions to specific things. We tried a bunch of different stuff and became passionate around Budo Brothers. The passion started a long time before that.

"Before Budo Brothers, we went on a trip together to Montreal. We had an absolute blast! It was so much fun, it was spontaneous, and we resonated together. We were filming things for skateboarding for Erik at one point. Whenever we hung out, it was exciting. It can happen at different moments or in different ways.

"Passion is something that can carry you through the hard times. You're excited; you want to learn and engage, and you go through it all. The feedback you read from your environment tells you that you are in line with something that is of value.

"When you help people, you are of service to them, and it feels good. It's a feedback loop. So when you combine those two things—you have an objective in your life that can propel you to grow and provide some service to others—you feel like you have some fulfillment.

"It's hard to feel like you're doing something fulfilling when you are by yourself. You are missing a component of passion—external feedback. You get this feeling with it that you are doing something right. That's what gives you a great sense of purpose."

Kyle's not wrong here. From my own perspective, when I write something that resonates with others, I'm at my happiest and feel like I'm fulfilling that purpose.

It is—exactly as he described—that component of something bigger that needs just a little bit extra to be in full focus. Your purpose is that silly image in the Magic Eye poster. It's there and in front of you, but it's only truly visible when you aren't focusing on only that single thing.

This shifts into a Japanese term called *ikigai*. Ikigai is a concept of merging together aspects of you to find what your purpose is. When you break it down, ikigai is a way of using something like a mathematical equation to find your purpose. The word *ikigai* translates roughly to "your reason for being."

Iki is "life."

Gai is "worth."

Ikigai is your life's worth. Your reason. The thing that inspires joy and gets you moving through life excited for every day.

It is comprised of the answer to four questions:

1. What do I love?
2. What am I good at?
3. What do others need?
4. What can I be paid for?

When all four of these things align, ikigai is discovered. This graphic will help you visualize ikigai:

We combine these questions to discover this "thing" about ourselves that resonates deep in our heart and in our head. I recently stepped through this exercise on my own, and I'll share my method and encourage you to go through your own as well. What we are looking for here is a through line. Something that makes sense when we tie the answers together. So I decided to list four answers to each question, in one or two words each.

1. What do I love?
    a. Storytelling
    b. Helping others
    c. Motivating others
    d. Writing

2. What are you good at?
    a. Communicating
    b. Storytelling
    c. Troubleshooting
    d. Teaching

3. What can you be paid for?
    a. Writing
    b. Mentoring
    c. Troubleshooting
    d. Teaching

4. What do others need?
    a. Honesty
    b. Fearlessness
    c. Confidence
    d. Perspective

My through line on these four questions very clearly boiled down to using my passion for writing to offer perspective and motivate others.

Makes sense that you're holding this book, doesn't it?

Take the time—scribble some notes down on a piece of paper and answer these questions on your own. Be honest about what you truly love, not what you want others to think of you. This is just you now, so let go and see where these answers take you.

I think you'll be surprised, and I can speak for Erik, Kyle, and myself in saying that we're excited for what you might uncover.

Openness and Letting Go

Ikigai is a concept that is rooted in change. This kind of self-discovery can be revelatory, but it has to come from an honest place, and it has to be from a perspective of allowing yourself to let go—temporarily—of how you've become you and finding more about what's really going on. It requires you to be authentic and open.

I wanted to dig in to the concepts of openness and change in terms of finding purpose, and Kyle and Erik both had a lot to say about this topic.

Kyle went first:

"It's this sweet spot. How you feel when you're in that flow state. Things feel easy. Time disappears. You know, when you're in it, you feel optimal. Everything feels just right. Your job is to try to balance those components to be in that flow state as much as possible. It's where you are most productive, you are at your happiest, you are doing purposeful work, and you're shining bright.

"That's how I view ikigai. It's where everything melts together to create this kind of purposeful happiness and bliss."

When we were sitting down together, and Kyle described it in this way, I immediately asked him to follow up. "If you have someone who is feeling purposeless, what would your advice be to help them find their ikigai?"

Kyle continued, "The steps of this are working out really well. You need to take ownership. You need to find your authenticity. You need that voice inside of you that gets muffled. When you're a kid, you think, 'I'm going to be this' or 'I'm going to be that.'

"You need to be in a place where you are still open enough to tune in to that dialogue. It's still going on in you! Whether it's through meditation or reflection, you have to start listening to what is inside. There's this voice in you that you've got to turn up the volume on. It starts off super quiet at the beginning. You have no idea what makes you happy or fulfilled. But there's a little voice inside of you that knows. Your job is to clear away all of the mess so you can hear that voice and that intuition.

"What prevents people from doing it is often the fear of trying and failing. You may not know what that voice is saying, but the only way to find it is to be an explorer and an adventurer. Try new things! Some will resonate, and some of those things you attempt will end up consuming your thoughts. You'll be thinking about it at night when you're trying to go to sleep, and it'll be on your mind in the morning. You'll be excited.

"People have made a living out of collecting Pokémon cards because they love it!

"Even if the reward isn't financial, having something in your life that gives you purpose—volunteering or creating art—will elevate every other thing in your life."

Erik ran with Kyle's last thought:

"You have to be open. If you're wandering and you're closed off, you're going to wander together. You're not open to new possibilities. You'll think things are just stupid.

"You'll say to yourself something like, 'Why would I make pottery? That's stupid.' That's a closed mind-set. But thinking, 'Hey I've never tried to make pottery before. I wonder if I'll like it?' That's being open."

Kyle interjected, "Oh, right! 'I'll never be able to make a living off making pottery!' You'll tell yourself lies to avoid what's new and different!"

Erik continued, "Exactly! The idea is now just dead on arrival because of your own bullshit! My brother struggled with this. He was struggling with what he wanted to do, so I gave him a morning routine to try. We went out to dinner because he was in a funk—hated his job and felt like he was wasting his time. So I told him that he had to find the challenge that would excite him.

"He was struggling with a decision lots of people struggle with. You have a family. You have to provide. You can't just chase woodworking as a passion because you have these other considerations.

"He was getting soaked under his own personal rain cloud over it, so getting a woodshop wasn't in the cards, but he enjoyed being engaged. It's a sticky situation trying to find that passion.

"He made a change and a conscious decision to go back to school. So he was open to going back to school for computer programming. He listened to his own internal reaction. It resonated. He took action and snapped out of the malaise. He took on the challenge and worked his ass off, and the gift was on the other side of that challenge, but only because he was open to a new reality—as scary as it was.

"We have a hard time writing off sunken costs. We have a personal history that colors our life. We think we're wasting our time, and we make our failures bigger than they really are and don't see them for the guideposts that they were in our life.

"It's so easy to be bitter, but my brother's story is an important lesson. He made it happen, and he's thriving!"

Kyle jumped in. "You have to kill your old self. You have to stop the pattern of your old self. The human you were up to this point in time that got you to this situation, you can take all of those lessons, but you have to detach from everything that old person has done. Let them go. Open up space for new things.

"If you put some of the old things back in because they are a benefit—fantastic. That's experience. But holding on to a bunch of old things that you've done in a new world may require letting go to become something new. Shed your skin and let go to create that new self.

"It's so hard. You love that person who got you to this point. But now you've got to let them go because it is time for you to level up and let go of some old habits."

In looking back at what Kyle is talking about here, it's easy to see a pattern emerging. Finding joy in large part requires letting go of the things that are anchoring you down to old patterns and old self. We get jealous when we see others having success. We spend time thinking about our terrible circumstances instead of accepting them and finding solutions. In terms of purpose, we hold on to this idea of what we once were, and without realizing, we are just shutting the door on how amazing we can become.

Be honest, be open, be authentic, and your ikigai will come into focus.

Searching for Fulfillment

We've all heard phrases like "it's darkest before the dawn" or "you can't have good without evil" or "after the rain comes the rainbow." Sometimes, focusing on negative outcomes helps us fully appreciate and understand the good ones.

After all, a week of sunny days is grand, but that first sunny day after a week of rain hits different.

It's in this spirit that I asked Erik and Kyle to describe searching for fulfillment, but to focus first on what happens when you don't. What happens when you are aimless and directionless and not searching for those things that fulfill you?

Erik chimed in.

"If you're not searching, you're coasting. You're floating. Ambivalent and careless. That's depression—when you don't care, and you're just thinking you want to let it all burn down.

"Not searching is a great way to return to the darkness. Part of fulfillment is the search itself. It's about the journey and not the destination. As soon as you think you've arrived, is that just it? It's over? You're done, and you can stop searching?

"No! It's continual! It's going to change, and new things are going to come up."

Kyle couldn't contain his enthusiasm for this topic. "This is the biggest part of finding purpose. Everyone skips this. It really never is about the destination. Once you acquire the thing you set out for, it doesn't matter. Purpose is enjoying the journey. Enjoying growing into the creative process. We say it all the time. Give us millions of dollars tomorrow, and we'd still be doing the same shit because this is what we enjoy doing.

"Once you find that thing where you enjoy the journey, the outcome stops mattering. You've found it! You've found fulfillment because you are in your craft. You are in line with your calling and your purpose—the divine, God, the Dao—you're in line with higher meaning and you can feel it.

"When you focus on getting to a place, you've already lost. Once you focus on enjoying the process of getting to the place, that's when you find fulfillment."

Erik continued, "You know, you're never going to arrive at the North Star. It's a guide, but not the destination. You use that as a guide, but you won't arrive at the North Star like, 'Oh shit, look at that. I finally made it to space! Must be time to go to the South Star!' It doesn't work that way."

(Author's note: These were hands down my favorite moments hanging with Erik and Kyle and discussing these topics. When they start bouncing the ideas back and forth, always adding more perspective. Kyle jumped back in at this point.)

"We had a goal of a million subs on YouTube, and it came to us way quicker than we'd thought. We got there, and it provided zero fulfillment. None at all. It was cool, I guess we're YouTubers, but it didn't make us feel fulfilled, and nothing changed. We love going and filming people and laughing and shooting—we enjoy that, and the result happened."

Erik was in agreement. "We also didn't wake up every day thinking, 'How are we going to get a million subscribers?' You know? We weren't fixated on anything. We just wanted to make things the people wanted to see. If you focus on the result and not the process, the result starts to lose meaning."

Kyle put this in focus in terms of the book you're holding right now:

"That's what I love about this book! We've barely focused on any kind of outcome. We're not sitting here thinking about stores and publishers—we just want to enjoy this process and make a good product."

I couldn't agree more with that final sentiment. And when I look back at my own ikigai exercise and think about that through line of using my own passion for writing and communicating to offer perspectives and motivate others, it makes so much sense.

When Kyle called me months ago and told me they wanted to write a book, that this project had to happen, and both he and Erik didn't want to do it unless I was involved, there was only one word on my mind.

"Yes."

I didn't know how this was going to happen. I didn't care to discuss any kind of payment or process. There was nothing like a contract or anything official. I'll be honest with you—at the time he called me, I was in a pretty dark place. My own work on fiction writing was stagnating. Every word felt like a knife fight in a back alley. Sitting down and throwing two hundred words down, something that should have taken me all of ten minutes, took an entire day.

That negative voice was screaming at me the day Kyle called.

"You won't finish the book! Say no!"

"You're not good enough to write this! You're going to fail!"

"Say no! You're depressed right now. Nothing is working. You're not ready!"

When my ikigai aligned, my instinct was "Fuck yes!" That's what passion and purpose do for you. It makes all of those little voices a little less impactful because something more important is right there for you. Opportunity, head, and heart were aligned, and those doubts stood no chance.

I placed my trust in their decision to work with me. I believed in the resonance we found in order to create something meaningful that aligned with our shared purpose. Now, this part of our journey is becoming part of your journey, and that's a remarkable turn of events. It's a perfect example of a search for fulfillment in perfect alignment with the journey.

It is about the journey. Sharing these thoughts and concepts with you isn't over when the book goes to print.

We're going to keep walking to that North Star. We just want you to start walking with us!

Observe Your Own Life

Observing your own life creates awareness. It creates awareness of how you feel. When you observe your life without being critical, you start acknowledging shit you might not want to acknowledge.

"For instance, I'm scared to leave my job. I don't want to admit that, but I am. I can ignore that because I know it's true, but by ignoring it, I'm not growing. I'm not getting past the fear. I stop learning. It's starting to fuck with everything in my life. Again, the only way is through.

"So observing your life will allow you to really understand where you're at with all honesty. It allows you to give yourself a real assessment but acknowledge the things that scare you or the things that excite you. And you know if it's true or not!"

It's particularly powerful hearing Erik's words as I write this right now. I've known these guys for years now, and I know it has been a real fight for them growing the business and holding down day jobs at the same time. Honestly, I don't even know how they managed it.

So I'm sitting here listening to Erik on audio and transcribing his thoughts that we recorded a few months ago. Last night I received a text from him:

That, my friends, is putting your money where your mouth is. It's incredible that I'm transcribing his words in this book at the same time that he's walking the walk. I knew that decision was weighing heavily on him. Kyle knew it. Erik himself admitted as much multiple times.

This is nothing short of inspiring, because all of us have struggled with change, following things we dream about and desire to do, and making our way.

I'm certain there was a lot of reflection on Erik's part coming to this decision, and he leaned on family and friends to guide him and put everything into per-spective. I'm sure many long showers of meditation had to happen, and to see him yank that pin out of the ground and move forward is a perfect encapsula-tion of what Joy-Jitsu is all about.

Ikigai cannot be denied.

Kyle puts this into perspective beautifully:

"When you look at yourself, you have to do it unattached to positivity and negativity. View it 'as is.' You can't say either, 'I'm so great' or 'I'm such a fuckup.' You have to eliminate those and say, 'This is what is happening.' It's like good journalism—you don't push any kind of a narrative. Not a narrative that people want to say about you, and not a narrative that you're inclined to say about yourself.

"This is where meditation helps. When I wake up in the morning, it's not like I'm not thinking of anything. I'm like, 'Oh shit, these negative thoughts are really in my mind. Good thing I caught it!' So if I'm feeling angry, I basically take an assessment. I say, 'Okay, I'm angry right now. Why? Can I do something to fix it?' That's viewing yourself as an observer.

"Don't think that you're losing anything, either. Some days, you just don't have it, and it's not 'taking an L' to admit it. You know you're tired, you know you don't have it, so the thing you need that day is to rest and recharge."

He's not wrong.

We hold ourselves up to these expectations, and they do a great deal of damage to us without us even realizing it. We think we have to push all the time; we have to hustle all the time. Every moment we're not moving forward, someone is moving past us. While that's true to some degree, it's also true that taking a break is part of progress. Knowing when you aren't at your peak and doing what your mind and body needs to be okay is progress in itself.

What happens if you don't eat?

What happens if you don't drink water?

What happens if you don't sleep?

Certain conditions have to exist in order for you to perform at your peak. Think about a race car. You can put the pedal to the metal, redline that engine, and pass all those suckers stopping in the pit to change their tires and fuel up. You don't want to waste a moment not moving forward, right?

That's until the race is halfway over, your tires have exploded, you're out of gas, the engine is blown, and you are getting passed by all those "suckers" who took the time to maintain and ensure they're working at peak. Those breaks you skipped because you were so concerned with pushing every available moment have now set you back into a position much worse than it should've been.

Maybe, instead of hobbling around the track, focusing on being ahead of everyone or not falling behind any perceived rival, you could have tuned that out. You would have been better served telling yourself, "I'm not going to have it in me to finish this thing if I don't take care of myself."

Taking the break and recharging is part of observing yourself and your tendencies, knowing when you are best served by an honest assessment. There's nothing wrong with recognizing that you've been burning yourself out.

That's you being an honest observer of your life and being your own advocate in terms of your needs.

I asked Erik and Kyle to finish this section up with some final thoughts on purpose.

Kyle went first:

"Stillness is medicine. We live in such a fast-paced world that we need stillness to counteract that. When we're so hyperfocused on finding our purpose, we burn ourselves out. Remember, purpose is always right beside you and in your immediate environment. If it wasn't, it wouldn't be your purpose, would it?

"It exists around you. It's your calling. You don't need to worry that it will find you. You just need to listen.

"Trust your purpose."

Erik had a warning about falling into a trap of purpose as a bargain for something:

"Purpose shouldn't be for a reason. It's not an exchange. It's not 'I need purpose because I want something.' It's a trap.

"We have to be careful of thinking about purpose as a means to an end. If there's a reason, there's a motive and an objective. It's inauthentic. Saying you need purpose because you need something makes purpose into an endgame, and guess what? That's not your purpose anymore. That's just work."

When we discussed purpose, I told Kyle about my journey writing my first book, *The Caretaker*. His response to what I said wrapped this all up and put a bow on it.

Here's what I told him:

"I was ready to invest two years into writing a book to make one sale and make no money. I would've been fine. It wasn't about anything other than getting to the finish line. My victory was saying that I set my mind to do something, and I accomplished it and loved the process and the storytelling. The fact that I wrote it and it resonated with other people and helped them really hit on my purpose. Deep down, I knew that would happen, not to any degree, though, because I try to have zero expectations.

"I wasn't here trying to be the next Stephen King or the next J.K. Rowling. I was just trying to be the first David Badurina to write this book."

Kyle's response:

"Isn't it funny, though, with that ikigai equation of yours? You have that passion about writing, but it's when you realized it helped other people—that service piece—that it came into focus as your purpose."

Be the observer, my friends. There are amazing things right beside you. Open your head, your heart, and your eyes, and enjoy your journey!

Your Journey Through the Dark— Leaving Darkness Behind

If purpose is the torch that has lit our way, growth is our progress in leaving behind what does not serve us. We were lost once, alone in the darkness, but we have managed to start a warming fire, light the way, and take steps forward toward something better.

This is growth.

Growth comes when you understand yourself and apply the proper perspective to your life and actions. It is the understanding and acceptance of where you are and how far you've come. Growth is the ability to continue to progress despite obstacles. By recognizing all that you've been through and how far you've come, everything becomes easier.

Unfortunate setbacks will happen, but growth shields you from losing your way. That torch is always alight, and though you may stumble, the path forward is now visible and clear.

In the growth section of this book, you'll learn about putting systems in place and approaching everything with a white belt mentality. We have to take a long, hard look at our cyclical behavior and adopt a mindset of focus. A new world is about to open its doors. When it does, the excitement you feel will be contagious to yourself and others.

We are leaving behind troubles that used to feel so heavy, becoming stronger with every step, and growing!

White Belt Mentality

Ah, the white belt.

I had a saying during my time running a dojo. Every student was familiar with it whether they were the youngest kid or the oldest adult.

When they took that first step on the mats, I handed them the white belt and said, "Here is your white belt. It is the only thing I will ever hand you that you haven't had to work to earn."

The white belt is that beginning. It marks the precise moment you are taking your first step on what is hopefully a long, fulfilling journey. The only thing you have to do is begin.

In fact, there is a very brief moment in time that's worth recognizing. It's the moment you realize you want to have a white belt in order to start something, but you haven't yet put it on and begun.

That's a special moment. There's a recognition that you don't know anything about what's to come. You have an open mind, and the next years can go in so many different directions—both positive and negative! But you make a decision, you place the belt around your waist, and many times that's the very first thing you learn—how to tie it.

These moments are special on a new journey in martial arts just as they are special in any new journey. Whether it's a career change, a relationship, moving to a new place, or having a child, you are in the beginning, and there are limitless paths you can walk based on the decisions you make and the work you put in.

One of the questions we get as instructors is, "How long does it take to get the next belt?"

That was my favorite question.

My answer was your typical, "It takes the same amount of time it takes to get your next belt."

Students who were hypercompetitive, always looking at those around them and wanting to treat the white belt like a chip on the shoulder, inevitably advanced slower than students who realized they weren't competing at all. Those who practiced and focused on their own path did the best. They may not have been the most skilled or gifted, but they knew the value in forward progress.

It is with these things in mind that I asked Erik to talk a little bit about putting on the white belt when Budo Brothers began:

"In order for Budo Brothers to be successful, we had to put on our white belts and admit that we didn't know anything when it came to e-commerce.

We had to learn how to do everything. We had to learn how to edit videos. We had to learn product development and filming. If this is really what we were going to dedicate ourselves to doing, we had to put on the white belts and go gain those skills. The only way to gain those skills is by getting on the mats, so to speak, and start training.

"Yeah, we looked like idiots at first, and everything felt foreign just like your first day in a new dojo. We had to roll with it and figure it all out. We were iterating our way to success!"

From my experience as described above, I wanted Kyle to follow up with some thoughts on ego. Because the moment you step on the mats—regardless of whether it's with a white belt or a black belt—ego must be checked at the door. It was always more difficult for the new ranks to drop it than those who have walked the path. So how does ego come into play with a white belt mentality? Kyle explains:

"For me, the white belt mentality was solidified when we came across Sensei Jay Creasy, who was our instructor in ninjutsu. At the end of every class, he would sit us down and have a conversation about life principles and skills. He calls it *san shin*. We talk about it in terms of having the heart of a three-year-old, or the mind of a child.

"To me, that's what the white belt mentality embodies. It's to view the world as though you were a young child. When you are a young child, you think you can fight everyone; you aren't scared to try anything and learn. I saw examples of this when I did some work with a school in Calgary. The young kids instantly jumped in and tried anything. They didn't care about what anyone thought of them. They were just free! They don't have social constructs preventing them from expressing themselves.

"I got to teach from elementary school up through grade twelve. Around ten years old, they start to feel embarrassment. That's where ego kicked in. It developed, and you start to think about whether you are good enough or deserve anything. We like to use the white belt mentality when we do everyday things. When we started Budo Brothers, we made a determination to look at it as if it was our first time and all we had to do was fuck around and find out.

"One of the biggest things that allowed us to succeed was when we got to a point where we were able to make mistakes but not have it ruin the business. In this process, mistakes are part of the game."

Erik jumped in: "You need to strike the right balance with experimentation. It's sort of a mad scientist experiment. You've got to mix around the different chemicals to the point where you progress, but there's not an explosion happening. When you're trying to do something that hasn't been done before you don't know what the outcome is going to be, but you have a hypothesis that you need to test. It's applying the scientific method, in a way. We thought, 'Hey, if we mix martial arts with a lifestyle, what would that reaction produce?' That's what we wanted to prove—that there was an underserved market. There was an entire community that hasn't been spoken to or brought together in a way that is accepting and growth-focused—a celebration of the martial arts lifestyle.

"Eventually, we started to prove it! Holy shit! There are so many like-minded people out there that have this similar mindset, that have the resonance of budo awakening something in their heart and soul."

Kyle's anecdote about ten being the age ego starts to creep in is spot on. One of the most difficult things I had to do as a martial arts instructor was create the conditions where adult students dropped their ego and would yell out a kiai when performing traditional kata. When you tell a little kid, "Okay, buddy, when you step and throw this punch I want you to scream, 'HAI!' Can you do that?" Their eyes widened! They'd look at me like, "Are you serious? I get to yell?"

The adults wouldn't do much more than squeak at first. Or they'd offer up a meek and semi-quiet "Hi." When it was particularly quiet, I'd just stand there smiling and say, "Hi," in return before explaining the expected volume.

But this is the nature of having that white belt mentality. When all of our adult bullshit gets caught up and gets in the way of us internalizing san shin, we prevent ourselves from learning and experiencing something new because we are too concerned with how we are perceived by others.

Growth is the gas pedal. Ego is pumping the brakes.

Erik added some thoughts about ego giving way to growth: "The point where I realized ego was getting out of the way was when I finally understood that Budo Brothers was not about us. I wouldn't care that I get my ass kicked on video every Monday night. It's not about me. If it was, ego would be involved, and I would care that I look bad. Budo Brothers has really helped me work on that, because when we first started, I was so concerned with looking bad. I took it personally if they didn't like the video. I internalized it. When all of that went away, I realized Budo Brothers has a life all its own. This is an awakening of other people. It's not about us!"

Kyle followed up that thought. "You can get so stale in your path. You can stop growing and stop learning. The fact that we are writing this book right now shows that we have a white belt mentality. It's a raw learning experience for all of us! You have to play and learn and add more skills because you want to look down the line and get to that black belt eventually. When you are a white belt, you are so eager diving into it all. When you can look at things like they are brand-new again, you grow faster.

"We are all sources of energy, you know? It's almost like all we are is a conduit to ideas that are floating around. All of these ideas are floating around, and everyone has access to them. There are infinite ideas flying everywhere. When you are able to turn on awareness to it and snatch one of them and become a conduit to where it becomes an actual thing on this planet, that's the divine way. You are not the idea itself—everyone has access to those ideas—you are the vehicle through which it manifests.

"Some people will react poorly to ideas. But even in the nastiest comment we receive, there is something to learn. For instance, for whatever reason, people do not like when people wear sunglasses in our videos, even if they're training outside. Our egos could've said, 'No, we want to wear sunglasses in the video,' but we accepted the criticism and decided not to do that.

"Everything needs a pressure test. You need to be able to detach your personal feelings and emotions from your work in order to hear criticism. That's why you have to detach your ego and adopt the white belt mentality. You have to be able to let go so you can get to the better thing and the better version—of you or whatever your endeavor is."

We can wrap up thoughts on the white belt mentality with these words of wisdom from Erik when we got him talking about dropping ego, trying new things, learning, and doing it again:

"Remember, Iteration is growth."

Consistent Persistency

There are two words we are going to focus on in this section.

Consistent.

Persistent.

Kyle jumped right into the topic of consistency: "I see consistency and focus as superpowers. Consistency—it's the ten-thousand-hour principle to become an expert. You don't do it; it works through you like a lightning rod. You have to show up, all the time. Some days it will be easy, some days it will be hard, some days you will hate it, and some you will love it. You have to show up all the time in order for that to work through you. If you only show up on the good days, you don't grow. In fact, you grow more on the days you suffer more."

Erik added to that thought. "Growing pains are a thing! You are by definition being constricted by your current state. If you are outgrowing, you are ready to get into a new shell."

Every once in a while, amidst our conversations, side stories, and joking, a curious question comes up. In this case—in terms of consistency—I wanted to know if Erik or Kyle could think of a moment when they recognized consistency as an ingredient in their success. Was there a moment when they realized they were constantly having to show up in order to grow?

Kyle answered, "This literally started before Budo Brothers. When Erik and I met and had a trip to Montreal. Without even knowing it, we filmed a great video of all the sights and sounds we were experiencing there. Budo Brothers didn't exist. We didn't even know we were both into martial arts. And we've just been refining that! Day in and day out, we create, we film, and we share experiences with people. Our products are designed around shared experiences. We just show up all the time and create moments and experiences for people. We were the architects of experiences, and that's something we felt we were really good at, and we just consistently do it every day.

"We literally do this every single day! Not a day goes by where we don't work on Budo Brothers. Every morning, we would jump on, figure out what our priorities are, strategize, then get to work. This is us getting our reps in. Our entrepreneurship reps! Every day."

In reflecting on Kyle's thoughts here, I can't help but think of people who struggle mightily with consistency. Sometimes it's hard to show up, and you'll want every excuse to be valid in order to not do it. It's work, or the kids, or you didn't sleep well, or you're tired, or it was a rough day. All of those little things are ways that your brain tricks you into packing it in for the day. That's when procrastination happens, and that's when you lose momentum, and lose something far more important.

Growth.

Without consistency, growth is incredibly difficult. So I asked Kyle to follow up on this because I wanted to know how he uses the concept of consistency in order to set himself up for more better days than bad days.

He explained, "It's all about my morning routine. Creating that routine was critical. It centers me every morning, and I just made it easy. It was to go for an hour walk every morning. The dog needs to go out anyway. Then I come back and work out, then I start my day. I get clear on my direction for the day, then I put in hours of work, and the rest I remain flexible."

Erik explained his most consistent habits in terms of being driven: "I feel like you have to have some kind of drive or desire. There has to be a driving force to fuel your willingness to consistently show up. Even when shit isn't going right! There has to be some kind of underlying purpose that you are working toward where you can consistently show up. There has to be a North Star that you are navigating toward.

"Growth requires pain. Look to nature. Nothing grows unless there is some ingredient of pain, some kind of challenge, or some adversity to overcome. That's what growth is!"

Kyle used some crystal-clear language to explain consistency: "If you eat shit for food every day, you will become a fat ass. If you study Spanish every day, guess what? You're going to be speaking Spanish soon. Whatever you consistently do, you become. If you can choose the consistent pattern that's going to produce the result you want, the quicker growth will happen!"

At this point in our conversation, I threw in the idea that consistency is part of an equation, but it's not the entire formula. In order for growth to truly happen, it requires persistence as well.

Think about it in terms of a straightforward goal—losing a few pounds.

I can take a walk two days in a row and each day walk a few miles. If I do that, I've had two days of consistency. If I stop on the third day because I looked at the scale and nothing changed, what I lacked was persistence. There's an element of faith to persistence, in that things will change if you keep at it.

Consistency is repeated behavior; persistence is progress. So let's throw it in a formula, shall we?

Consistency + Persistence = Growth

Kyle brought it home in terms of how persistence requires some faith: "Persistence is faith. You can't see the result. You have to believe that what you are doing is going to get you to the goal, so it is tied to faith. Consistency is more of a metric. You're saying, 'I did this thing *x* number of days in a row.' In order to grow, both of those need to happen."

If you want to grow into something—whatever that "thing" is—you need both consistency and persistence. Consistency is the act of accomplishing that behavior that is going to eventually lead to you achieving a goal, and persistence is drive. Think of persistence as the armor in your mind that says, "Even though I've had a crap day, if I keep at this, I cannot fail."

Which brings me to push-ups.

When I first started martial arts as an adult, I was about seventy pounds overweight. A true chonk of a human being that got used to desk jobs and zero physical activity.

Unless you count eating.

That first day, my instructor asked me to bang out as many push-ups as I could in one shot.

I stopped at nine.

To be honest, I was embarrassed. Kids were doing more push-ups than I was, and I ended up determined to put everything I could into training both physically and mentally.

I studied hard, practiced constantly, and worked on my physical ability with a furious passion. Now, I was a martial artist as a kid as well (Tang Soo Do for those curious). So I had always retained flexibility and an understanding of body control from those earlier days.

Two years later, I tested for my black belt in American Kenpo. That test was grueling. Five-plus hours, kata, sparring, weapons work, and physical exhaustion during hours of self-defense drills.

And one thousand push-ups. Twenty-five or fifty per set sprinkled into everything else we were asked to do.

The push-ups were the least difficult part of that test. And the reason they were the least difficult is because I invested two years of my life doing push-ups every day (consistency) and never giving up when I was tired or having a poor day (persistence).

Who do you want to be? Do you want to be that person who grows? That person in your circle of friends and family that has the reputation as someone who is so tenacious that, regardless of obstacles, still moves forward? That's what consistency and persistence gets you. If you lack persistence, you are the person that does the things until the things are difficult. That's a simple case of lacking faith that the desired result will happen. If you lack consistency, well, you can have all the drive in the world, but you aren't setting yourself up to succeed because you are not showing up every day to make it happen.

If there is a secret in there somewhere as far as how to grow as a human being, it's to embrace both of these concepts.

Consistency + Persistence = Growth

Cyclical Behavior

Have you ever in your life thought, "This again?"

Was it something you did? Was it a pattern that was repeated or a failure that cropped up again for whatever reason?

I want you to think about the cycle that took place in order to create that circumstance. Cycles can be good, bad, or perfectly neutral. We have four seasons on this planet (unless you're in Hawaii or Nunavut, in which case you can pretty much expect some of the same stuff year-round). That cycle of seasons is normal and natural for our planet because of our cycle of orbiting the sun, which is in its own cycle of travel through the Milky Way.

What is not a natural cycle is repeated failure. That's a cycle of behavior patterns, and behavior can change, leading to a change in whatever cyclical pattern you fell victim to.

Accepting unbreakable cycles as something you cannot change (death, the seasons, aging) and refusing to stay within the confines of breakable cycles within your control (what you eat, your state of mind, your physical activity) is yet another key to growth.

It was clear during my conversation with Kyle that this was one of his favorite topics.

He explained: "We are patterns. We will always continue in a circle and receive the same problems until you solve or break free to the next level or set of problems. You beat the boss on that level, and then you get to the new boss and the new set of challenges.

"When you are a toddler and you're learning how to walk, running isn't even a concept yet. Then you learn to walk, and you're wanting to do backflips!"

Erik jumped in: "This is the beauty of mankind! We are always pushing the boundaries of what is possible. And here's what's so fucking mind-blowing about it—if you look at any of mankind's pursuits, what is possible now would be unfathomable twenty years ago!

"Take any area—go watch gymnastics in the 1968 Olympics, and what they thought was miraculous is what's being taught in high school gym right now! It's so trippy because our hardware hasn't changed! We have the same evolutionary body, so why is it that we are now capable of doing more as a human species?

"I believe it is in our genetic code to take the risk. We push the boundaries. We go to the limits of what's possible. That is growth. It's continual, we're always growing as a species thanks to the prior generation's discoveries. We come along with a fresh perspective, expand on that lifetime of experience, and continue to push things forward with our own innovations.

"It's continual evolution of what it means to be human. You can point to any endeavor and see that evolution and unstoppable perpetual growth as a product of what it means to be human."

I can't resist throwing in an anecdote about a hugely influential person personally to both Erik and me, and in pop culture in general.

Tony Hawk.

I was never a real skater, but I knew how to land an ollie and a kick flip when I was younger. Erik was a serious skater throughout his life. I was, obviously, a massive fan of the video games—*Tony Hawk's Pro Skater*. I never looked at handrails the same after that game, and when I picture the grounds of a high school, I hear Rage Against the Machine's "Guerrilla Radio" playing in my head.

I bring up Tony Hawk to illustrate a point about cyclical behavior and breaking boundaries.

Skateboarding had existed for decades by the time the late 1990s and early 2000s rolled around. Something previously thought unfathomable, however, happened in 1999.

Tony Hawk hit a 900. That's 2.5 revolutions (900 degrees) jumping off a skateboard ramp and landing back on the wheels afterward. This was a trick thought impossible to, well, the world.

Until he did it. Now he practiced and tried and tried and likely broke his foot a few times in the process of attempting something that was beyond the boundary of comprehension.

He was consistent in his practice for years and flexed such persistent tenacity that he knew he'd land the trick, and he made it happen and blew minds in the process.

Incredible, right?

Do you know who Tom Schaar is? Probably not.

Tom Schaar was twelve years old in 2021 and landed a 1080.

A twelve-year-old, standing on the shoulders of a giant, breaking the boundary that was once seen as impossible, and setting a new bar. And he wasn't the only one to do it! A few months after his 1080, a skater by the name of Gui Khury landed a 1080 during an X-Games competition.

It is these kinds of achievements—attainable only through tenacious growth—that make humans ache to reach the stars and draw on the passion to constantly exceed expectations and answer questions.

Achievement is wired in your DNA. You were not meant to be stuck in a cyclical pattern, doing the same task over and over, day in and day out. You are designed to grow!

Erik was beyond enthusiastic about this topic: "What about the four-minute mile? Unfathomable to run a four-minute mile! Then someone did it. What, all of a sudden—just because someone with the audacity to break the four-minute mile—makes it okay for tens of thousands of people to break that boundary?"

Kyle answered: "As soon as you lose the belief that it's impossible, it becomes possible. That's exactly what happened. When I think of these cycles, I think you are a trap within the cycle. The cycle gives you problems to pass. You are unaware of the problems at the start. If you have something showing up in your life consistently, it's because of a pattern. Bad relationships are a great example. If you are consistently suffering through bad relationships, you're stuck into a pattern, and you need to get into a new set of habits and behaviors.

"You have to destroy old patterns and old ways of living to level up and become something new. You have to kill that old self and those old ways of doing things to create the space to grow into something new.

"It's most uncomfortable and puts the most pressure on you when you are right about to break out of that cycle and into something awesome. The problems and challenges change, but you leave that shell that you've outgrown and move into a new shell that you grow into and then out of again. That's the cycle.

"Good times don't always roll, either. There are moments in time where you are amassing success.

You ride the wave for everything it's worth, but those moments in time never last. Eventually the wave dies, and you find yourself on shore. So you work hard, expend energy and effort, and paddle back out to where the waves come. Then all of a sudden the perfect wave shows up again, and you ride it again all the way to shore. Each time, you improve and learn and take advantage of the next great wave better than you ever could have imagined."

All of this raised a very interesting question in my head, so I asked Kyle to follow up.

"What do you tell someone," I asked, "that is stuck in a cycle and can't recognize how to get out?"

Kyle explained, "The problem is, when you are stuck there, it is subconscious. You can't see the issues clearly. Right now, we are all stuck in patterns that are preventing us from reaching the next tier of success. We don't know. That's where a good mentor can help, because they can observe and see it in you through their own experience. Having someone to talk to is a huge thing, and that consistent pursuit of that end result.

"And drop that ego! Have some humility and listen to the people close to you. Other voices see you and care about you, and sometimes you aren't ready to hear the honesty because you aren't close enough to the breaking point of that cycle. Until that moment arrives and it's in front of you, the advice of others won't help you break the cycle. Sometimes, though, it's the last push to break that cycle when you need it most."

Erik wrapped up this advice with a simple statement: "You can't break the cycle until you see it, and you can't see it until you observe yourself doing it. You are unconscious until you can be your own observer. Then you say, 'Why the fuck am I doing this?'

"And that's when you break the cycle. That's when you grow. Completing that cycle takes focus. It's difficult to do, and when you do it, it pays all the dividends."

Putting Systems in Place

My background is in technical work—troubleshooting and relational database design and development. It's incredibly boring most days. Like accounting, it's not exactly the type of work that is constantly throwing fun challenges and opportunities your way.

There is data. You organize the data according to a set of rules. You then update and maintain the data.

It's not exactly Cirque du Soleil during my day-to-day work. I'm not getting launched out of circus cannons and expressing myself through the art of high-flying trapeze. There is data. I get it organized and clean. I move on.

Now, it pays the bills, and certainly there are some data "puzzles" that come my way that make it a little more interesting, but overall it's straightforward logical work. To do this, I employ different coding languages or software to make it all function the way it should. When someone says the word *system*, I think of operating system or a coding language or software application of some kind.

I don't think about drinking water. So this conversation came out of left field; my familiarity with the word *system* was purely technical. Kyle explained how he and Erik use systems in terms of growth. When he explained it this way, it opened my eyes.

A system doesn't have to simply be technical. It's merely something you put in place to address an area of need or weakness.

Here's how Kyle explained using a system in order to explode the growth of Budo Brothers:

"A system is similar to technology or a way that you can deal with your weaknesses and make things more efficient. For us, we are very creative. We are very good at adapting. We are terrible at organization and structure.

"Erik and I can sit here and talk for years about being more organized, but organically it's just not us. It'll get better, but the degree that it will get better is very slow. So in order to fill that void, or that need, you need to have a system in place to replace that. Generally, that's some kind of resource. In our case, that was hiring Tiffany. And literally right after we hired her, our business doubled. We just had our highest-grossing month! It was all because we put that system in place.

"So you put that system in place in order to fill the void. If you don't like drinking water, put a water bottle by your bedside that helps you to drink the water. You put an action in place to garner a specific result."

Systemizing your water intake seems like an excessively professional way to say "drink more water," but that's not the point. The point is, whatever it is you're struggling with that is holding you back from growth needs some assistance. That system is you being honest with yourself and some of the things that may be shortcomings and taking the steps to delegate that task in a way that sets you up for more growth and more success.

You can't do that with ego in the way. You can't do that by being a control freak. You do that by observing your behavior, recognizing where you need to address something, and allowing it to be addressed so you can be at your best.

Erik explains: "Growth requires humility. It requires the ability to look at your own flaws. You have to be able to recognize your weaknesses and get over yourself to understand that you have a void that needs to be filled. It's not easy to do."

Kyle jumped in: "It shows up for me in the entrepreneurial space. Growth in entrepreneurship is literally all about creating systems. It's the nature of the whole game. Look at McDonald's. It could be one guy flipping burgers. But if you create a line of people, you can produce more burgers and unlock growth.

"Systems unlock the ability to do more with your time.

"You systemize the redundancies of your actions so that you can take on more or higher producing tasks."

This has been true in business and industry for more than a century. Henry Ford created the assembly line. Sure, you can have fifteen people tripping over themselves trying to put together one car at a time from start to finish, but by creating a system where one person can do an expert's job on one task and move the car down the line, it creates the conditions for more growth and more output.

The workers back in 1913, however, got bored. They tired of doing the same task over and over, plus the pressure of doing it efficiently before the car moved down the line.

Henry Ford needed another system to address the issue.

What did he do? He cut their work hours and doubled their wage, introducing something called the five-dollar workday. Employees would be paid a great wage (at the time, obviously) of five dollars, and they'd work slightly less hours. Most thought Ford would be bankrupted by this move.

What did that system do?

Skilled mechanics from all over the country descended on Detroit looking for work because of the great wages and shorter work hours. Henry Ford ended up attracting top-notch workers, and by having them work less hours, he was able to create a third shift. That third shift turned Ford into a twenty-four-hour operation. The powerhouse of high-production assembly line vehicles was born. Vehicles became cheaper to produce, thus cheaper to purchase, and decades later, you're hopping in your minivan taking your daughter and her nine best friends to a Taylor Swift concert.

Ford benefitted from this system. Customers benefitted. Employees were able to provide a great life for their families, and the culture changed forever. Why? Because someone recognized a need for a system, implemented it, then did it over and over again.

Thank you, Henry Ford!

By the way, Max Newgar invented earplugs in 1907. So if you need a system to be able to attend a Taylor Swift concert with your daughter and nine of her best friends without subjecting yourself to the full volume of it all, you can thank Max.

Kyle continued, "Systemization allows us to focus on what we do best. The best use of our time is not focusing on accounting. We systemize that role so we can put our effort into marketing and customer acquisition. When we find a higher, more potent use of our time, we systemize what we can to maximize our output and to produce more value. It's all about creating conditions for growth.

"This all ties back to it being bigger than you. No matter what you think it should be, real life has a different opinion. We may think something is going to be the absolute best, and we'll put it out, and it flops. Listening is the hardest thing to do, but you accept criticism. You may want to do it your way and have all the control over it, but it can be paralyzing. Systems create an easy way to work with people. What you are creating is a way for someone to work with you.

"You may write a book, but you work with an editor to polish it up if you're not as skilled with editing. An editor will do better, so you use the editor. You want them to be better, and sometimes that's hard because of your ego. You need to work with people that are better than you at things. You have to work with people better than you."

"And you know what?" added Erik. "If you really want to grow, you have to be able to admit that you need to work with people that are better than you at certain things.

"That can be a real kick in the dick."

Stop Playing GTA

Many of you know what GTA is the moment you see those three little letters next to each other. If you're a gamer, you know the *Grand Theft Auto* franchise because it is an integral part of video gaming culture and history. Upon seeing it in this context, you may be thinking, "Huh, I wonder what Joy-Jitsu has to do with a game where you literally rob, steal, shoot people, and set prostitutes on fire?"

Joy-Jitsu has nothing to do with any of that, of course. At least not outside of a very roundabout way. I'm sorry to disappoint you, I guess?

But there is a concept and a multitiered parallel in here that's worth exploring. I swear, gentle reader, I am going to tie this all together. First, let's talk about cool shit like lasers.

Growth takes focus, and to Erik, focus means lasers!

He explains: "When I hear the word *focus*, I think of the ability to melt rocks using the sun through a lens. A lens—a giant magnifying glass—can concentrate the dispersed energy of the sun into one location like a laser. That has the ability to melt fucking rocks! When you can focus all of that energy to a single target, it's how you create lasting effects and big results.

"Huge achievements are brought into reality this way. Dispersing light is not how you start a fire. It takes a focal point to concentrate that energy to the point where ignition takes place. A flowing garden hose isn't capable of much more than watering the lawn. But, that same volume, if brought to a narrow enough focal point, can cut through hardened steel in a matter of seconds. It's about concentration.

"That's the challenge of living in a world that is full of distractions! This is where the power of focus can cut through steel, but it's the hardest thing to do."

Kyle added: "Time is the most valuable asset any of us have. It is represented in today's world as attention. Because time is so valuable, no matter what you do or where you go, something or some device is always trying to steal that time. That's what society values because it is the most precious thing.

"Time is stored in money. When you are able to focus, you are taking control of your time."

Erik jumped in: "The world is designed to steal your time! When you steal something, it's called theft! There are thieves that are stealing your time!"

Kyle agreed: "Time is stolen through attention. Your phone notifications. You thinking about some thought that doesn't matter. All of these things are stealing your time and your attention. Focus is you taking control of your attention and time and putting it into a place where you know it's going to be valuable."

You need to look at and understand time for the finite resource it is. You are born, and from that moment, you have a certain amount of time on this planet. Doomscrolling cat videos on Instagram is literally taking your life away.

Think of the time you have as currency—really the only currency that matters sitting in a fictional "time account" at a local Time Bank.

You can never add more time to that bank. Someday, it will run out. The balance will only ever go down, minute after minute, day after day.

Would you willingly allow someone access to your time account to deduct some of those minutes away? Would you install an app on your phone that gives you nothing of value but deducts time from your time account every time you open it?

Would you press that button that says "Allow Access" if some random programmer in Kazakhstan wanted to put an app on your phone that lets you move little jewels around on a screen in order to take minutes from your life in exchange for a fake in-game currency?

If you are sitting at the dinner table with your family, would you take a call from that Kazakhstan programmer and allow them to pull you away from your dinner table and your family for five or ten minutes each night?

I'm not trying to be excessively dramatic, but when you are spending your last few hours on earth, will you be thinking about wishing you had a few more minutes with your kids, or will you be thinking about having a few more minutes doomscrolling parkour fail videos on TikTok?

When I brought these points up to Erik and Kyle, I phrased it this way and explained it like a video game literally sapping precious moments of your life away.

That's GTA.

Grand Theft Attention.

Kyle ran with it. "Your life is long and short at the same time. When you're young, you think you have so much time. Then all of a sudden you're older, and time becomes this weird thing that flies by. You can tell a person when tomorrow comes you have a day to live, or you have fifty years, and they will live their life differently according to how much time they have left.

"We don't know the parameters, though. But we often act as if we have forever."

Make no mistake, I am a gamer, and I enjoy playing video games as part of my downtime and rest. It's engaging in a different way, and I enjoy the storytelling and the occasional challenge. For me, that's how I focus on decompressing and getting some needed rest for my brain. Like anything, it's best in moderation. Playing video games all day, every day without seeing the outside world is a terrible idea. Knowing ways you can manage yourself, your energy, and your mood is important.

You can be a carpenter and be thrilled with woodworking every moment. That doesn't mean that taking a shower is a waste of time building your woodworking business. Time with your family, time to eat, time to decompress and give your body a rest—all of these things are critical uses of your focus.

"Working vacations" are not critical uses of focus. That's the hose spraying everywhere. When you are on vacation, limiting everything except enjoying time alone or with family is the most important thing. You focus on your vacation, so you are better focused when you are back at it.

Kyle continued: "There's an epidemic of people wanting to be in a different place from where they are. Your brain is in so many places other than the task at hand. You are thinking about a movie you saw, or something you have to do, or bills you have to pay, or what you're going to do next week. If you could drop all of those attention-eating things and focus on one task, you'd be so much better for it.

"You can't only focus on one singular thing the whole time, right? You burn out. Other things need your attention. Can someone truly multitask? Or is that bullshit? Because you can only truly do one thing at a time, so you're just doing a whole bunch of one-things at a time. You have to focus on one thing at a time, anyway, so do that.

"As humans, we want to get things done faster. Focus decreases the time it takes to get things done because your attention is not split. It allows you to level up faster than other people. You are able to focus, complete a cycle, get something done, and move on to the next level. It increases the speed at which you can grow."

Erik added: "Focus is the sprint. You get to the finish line faster. You'll be gasping for air because you turned on the afterburners, but you're giving it all you got. You're maxing this bitch out! Now, that's going to get you there fast, but it's not going to take you the distance. You can break your engine just like we have broken our business, which required us to take it all back to the garage and rebuild it because we drove too fast and broke it. We needed more torque. So we do that, rebuild it, rev it, break it again, bring it back and go faster. Growth is figuring this out. Growth is iterating and growing.

"So choose your focus! We get to choose what we focus on. It's a choice. We are given a smorgasbord of shit to be concerned about, but you get the choice of what you get to focus on, so choose accordingly. That lens that focuses the sunlight—you are the one who gets to direct where it is pointing.

"Remember those books? Choose Your Own Adventure books? Weren't they the best? To reach the mummy's tomb, you have to figure out which path to take! And just like your life, that novel was based on the decisions you made and where you chose to focus. The things you choose to pursue, everything. Where you decide to devote your gifts, passion, and purpose determines the path you walk.

"Life is choosing your own adventure!

"And this book! This book has the attention of a reader right now, and it is our responsibility to match their investment of time to something that gives them amazing value in their life moving forward. It has to be returned with interest. If I'm going to take the asset you have, and you're going to give me that asset, I need to give it back with a return on that investment. We need to be a dividend. Our goal as Budo Brothers is to inspire and educate. We provide value, and that's the hack. If you're going to engage in Grand Theft Attention, you better have a return on that investment.

"We provide value when our customers provide attention. Our effort is the interest on that investment to give you something you didn't have before this interaction. We provide value in exchange for your attention. That value is something that will help you grow.

"Stupid videos about celebrities offer no return on investment. We make sure that everything we do will. That's just honoring your focus."

In the spirit of Erik's closing remarks on growth . . .
To continue your journey escaping the deep, dark woods, turn to the next page!

Your Journey Through the Dark— Pacing Your Path

The ebb and flow is a constant reminder of the Joy-Jitsu journey. When we progress to this point, and we've grown and done it with purpose, we can push ourselves too far.

In our scenario, we have lit our metaphorical torch and walked the path of growth, attempting to no longer feel lost and alone.

Can we burn out?

Survival skills are more than just running headlong into any circumstance before you. Knowing when to stop and breathe is just as critical as knowing where to go and how to get there.

What we want to avoid is burnout. Running through the woods, we will fall, get scraped and cut, twist an ankle, and risk being more lost than we were before. Taking our time to collect ourselves, resting, and focusing on every aspect of our journey will allow us to make steady progress.

You know the story of the tortoise and the hare, right? The tortoise is the hero.

Be the tortoise.

Recognizing the power of equilibrium puts you on a stable path to move forward in your life, and that's what the section on balance will bring into focus. Let's keep making our way out of that dark forest, but let's do so with deliberate steps and a keen eye for how to best navigate our way to safety, comfort, and success!

Truth Lies in the Middle

At this stage in our journey of Joy-Jitsu, we have made amazing progress, but it all comes with some caution. And the cautionary aspect of Joy-Jitsu is all about maturity.

Balance is maturity in your journey. It's knowing your strength (perseverance), counting your blessings (gratitude), understanding who you are (authenticity), being certain of why you do what you do (purpose), and knowing the right way forward (growth).

We have many tools in our toolbox at this point, but without a little maturity, we can easily be thrown off our path. As with any journey, you must always expect to stumble and fall. Maturity is what allows you to step back and understand that you must pace yourself properly in order to achieve great things.

If you are going to invite more joy into your life, burning yourself out is not the way to do it!

When I ushered in this topic, Kyle told me the story of two wolves:

"The story of two wolves is an old fable. An elder is teaching his grandson about life. 'A fight is going on inside of me—a terrible fight between two wolves. One is evil and angry, resentful, full of ego and self-doubt. The other is good. He is peaceful, benevolent, and compassionate. The same fight is going on inside of you and everyone else.'

"When the boy asked him which wolf will win, the elder replied, 'Whichever you feed.'

"Both good and evil exist within you. It's the yin and yang, good and evil, light and dark, joy and pain. Everything has a counterbalance. I often say that your gift is also your curse or tends to torment you in some way.

"Knowing that there's a balance going on inside of you is so important in understanding that anything you do has a cost. You work very hard, but there's a cost of time. You can have joy, but there will also be pain."

It's a wonderful way to think about your life as a whole. You can enjoy sunny days and dark days, but those sunny days just hit different when it's been raining and cloudy for a week. Balance puts every-thing into perspective. The mature perspective is focusing on that truth that lies within the gray. Not the best of times, not the worst of times, but the in between.

Erik expanded on these ideas.

"I had a realization a long time ago that every person has the ability to recognize truth. I started thinking about that—how can we recognize something that we don't know? In order for you to recognize something, you have to know it. If I'm going to recognize a friend in a public place, I have to know what that friend looks like, right?

"When somebody speaks truth, you recognize it instantly, and it just vibrates something inside of you. It's powerful. That recognition of the truth requires us to already know what that truth should look like, and that dust of life makes it seem less clear. Sometimes it just takes that external nuance of the way someone said it to understand how true it is.

"That was a trick for me—we all already know the truth. When we recognize that, it just reminds us that it's a fundamental truth."

Kyle jumped on that idea:

"The yin and yang is the ultimate symbol of balance. Sometimes you live in the black areas, sometimes in the white areas. In your life you flow between the two. What happens when you mix black and white?

"You get gray.

"The truth lying in the gray is understanding that in your life you aren't always going to be good or always going to be evil. You'll be combinations of many things. Balancing those out allows you to be the best version of yourself.

"No matter who you are, you're going to have demons. There's a piece of you that doesn't do good things. In psychology, it's called your shadow. It's whatever aspect of you that brings you toward negative light. The way to counter that is to add the opposite.

"When you are deep in your shadow, you add white to get to the gray. The opposite is true too! If you're nothing but constant humor and hilarity, you need to bring yourself back to earth in order to function in reality.

"Keep yourself in check!

"You can't be working too much and ignoring family. You can't be always with family and not working. The answer is somewhere in the middle. You feel it when you're out of balance."

So what happens when you allow yourself to get too high on the highs, and how do you balance it? Also, what happens when you are consumed and overtaken by the lows?

Erik answered, "The danger of irrational exuberance is that it's exactly that. It feels so fucking good, this alluring feeling of excitement and thinking nothing could possibly go wrong. But that's an imbalanced state. It's the rose-colored glasses that cannot detect threats.

"Even acknowledging the threats is going to mess with that amazing feeling you're having. I look at my own experience—when I wanted to leave my cushy engineering job to go build a skateboarding app, I was jacked up! I thought, 'This doesn't exist! I have a programmer guy ready to go!' I was irrationally exuberant, and I wasn't looking at the glaring holes that had to be addressed for that venture to be successful.

"Spoiler alert. I ignored everything! It dampened that amazing feeling that I had. I was so ready to go and thought it was so great, but I wasn't tempering or balancing it. I wasn't being brought back to earth, because I was so high on that feeling that I got blindsided by everything I ignored. By confronting those trials, it's a buzzkill, and it knocks down your dopamine."

This hits precisely on my point about balance being linked to maturity. So I asked Erik, that when those feelings happen now, what does his inner monologue say?

"I try to break my own ideas. I try to challenge that idea. Challenge the concept. I try to challenge it because through that challenge you become stronger. It's like working out! The muscles grow because we are challenging them with weight. I want my ideas to be challenged. If I'm super pumped about a product, I want the challenge to it. Feedback lets me work through it to make it stronger."

Kyle jumped in on this answer: "One thing that Erik and I have worked hard at is constantly challenging each other. Perfect example—we're bringing out the Hood-Gi and he was all, 'This is gonna be dope!'

"So I said, 'Prove to me that it's gonna be dope!' And that challenge let us work through the product and make something awesome. Sickest hoodie ever. But you have to let your ego out of the way in order to accept that feedback and work through it. Even with our business, we really just build it to break it and grow stronger."

Erik finished off this thought: "Challenge brings around balance. Looking through the lens of an entrepreneur, you have all these ideas, and it's not balanced. The challenge brings back reality. That's how something evolves, grows, and becomes tempered."

This brings me back to one of my favorite pieces of Joy-Jitsu—observing your own thoughts.

Observing your own thoughts isn't just a technique to move through negative thoughts such as, "I'm experiencing anger right now" or "I'm experiencing sadness."

It's an incredible tool to balance yourself. "I'm experiencing a lot of enthusiasm about this!" When you can observe that high, you're able to say, "Okay, I can't be irrational about this? How do I put a challenge to this idea to make sure it's legit?"

You can still retain all of the enthusiasm and accept and work through the challenges to those ideas.

That's how you stay mature.

That's how you stay balanced.

That's how you create positive iterations!

The Music of Life

When I was a kid, I wanted to be a rockstar.

The only problem with that boldest of dreams was this little thing called "talent." The only way I'm able to carry a tune is if I physically move a compact disc from the case to the player. When I sing, young mothers hold their babies' ears and back away with horrified looks on their faces. When I tried singing a solo in fourth grade, the music teacher listened and then said, "Okay. Don't."

But still, I tried. I learned how to play some piano and eventually learned guitar and bass. I practiced and improved my skills, and in high school I tried out for—and successfully joined—my high school jazz band. We were actually a great band with a great teacher. Second place in the state of New Jersey in 1993!

I listened to every type of music imaginable to better understand the structure of song and melody and to adopt things I loved into my own skill set. With guitar, I was a huge fan of older music. I loved Yes, Led Zeppelin, and King Crimson. When I was honing my bass-playing skills, I dove into modern Afro-Cuban jazz and seventies funk. I was constantly listening to James Brown, Tower of Power, and George Clinton.

Nothing can inspire a white boy from suburban New Jersey like Bootsy Collins! Astronomical!

Through all of that, though, I ended up picking up a really bad habit in my playing.

Too many notes.

My band teacher at the time was listening to me horsing around on the bass after practice and simply said, "Play the pauses."

I'd never heard that phrase before, and on asking him what it was, he explained that the space between each note is just as important as the note itself. The quotation—as best as my research reveals—would be attributed to a classical pianist named Artur Schnabel.

Here's the full quote:

"The notes I handle no better than many pianists. But the pauses between the notes, ah, that is where the art resides."

I have thought about that quote consistently since I was eighteen.

Some of the greatest communicators history has ever known were able to pause their thoughts and speech—not for dramatic impact but because the message requires it.

You see, if you just hop on an instrument and keep playing notes, you'll find that what comes out is just a jumble of melody with no real purpose or message behind it. But those little pauses—treating them as if they are just as important as the notes themselves—that's when magic happens.

And this applies to life as well.

You may be in a business meeting and a negotiation may be critical to the survival of your company. Just blurting out every thought and assaulting the other side with facts and data ends up muddying the water. Playing a pause—letting a critical or impactful thought hang in the air for a moment to let it sink in—then moving forward with concise follow-up—that's what creates impact in messaging.

It's no different in finding balance in your life. Running yourself ragged 24/7 is a great way to muddy everything. Nothing has an impact because you are dispersed and throwing everything out to try to make something stick. Taking your time, studying, and being thoughtful with your actions ends up giving your actions more impact than they had before.

Kyle sums this up beautifully in terms of life:

"If you were to picture your life as a symphony. In a symphony, you will have high notes and low notes. When the notes are high, everything is great and euphoric, but within the symphony there are low notes—like darkness, pain, and sadness.

"If you only lived within one note, there is no balance. When you put it all together, you have highs and lows. You flow between different states and experience all of it in a beautiful piece of music. Your life becomes a symphony. Understanding that life has highs and lows means understanding that there's a state of balance. You don't become too attached to either peak or valley. You are the entire song."

When everything is going your way and you are active and engaged, those high notes are singing! But they won't always sing. Just like any incredible piece of music, your life will take a turn toward something slower, darker, and quieter.

And that is part of the music.

When those dark notes and minor keys hit, it can feel like that symphony is a coming storm on the horizon. The clouds grow dark, the rain starts, and all you can do is try to hold on.

Between all of those highs and lows, there lie the pauses. Those times where life is moving apace, and you are getting through the routine. It is within that space where you are able to see and understand that you are balanced. You don't have the euphoric highs of the highest notes and frantic score, and you don't have the depressing lows of those drawn-out minor melodies. You are in the pauses, able to observe and understand that both the exuberant melody and melancholy dissonance are going to wash over you at some point.

What I learned and applied so many years ago was that observance. I am able to recognize those notes when they are approaching, and I use that time between—the pauses—to set myself up to weather both of those storms.

As Kyle so magnificently put it, "You are the entire song."

Play the pauses, my friend. Be the music of life—the high notes, the low notes, and the pauses in between.

That's balance.

Equilibrium

One of the things I'm most fascinated by is how people overcome negative thoughts. We all have them—those moments of doubt or self-pity. There are always moments of doubt or self-pity. People who have a supremely positive mindset seem to handle those thoughts with great skill. So in thinking about the topic of balance and more specifically equilibrium, I imagine a boat being tossed around in rough seas.

That boat may list from side to side, but it's not capsizing. In fact, a skillful captain is able to steer that vessel at just the right angle to lessen the impact of the waves that are approaching. Kyle is one of the most positive people I've had the pleasure of knowing, so I asked a direct question.

"When you feel like those times are really tough, how do you find equilibrium?"

"When I see negativity and darkness, I see it as a monster that keeps consuming. When you're in the depths of it, you feel like you're down so deep that you almost want to pile more of it on. You're like a magnet for negativity. When you're in hard times, you almost want more hard times. You want to soak in the pity. You don't exercise, and you don't feel good, and you can fall into destructive behavior because it's a spiral.

"Once you can have awareness of that downward spiral—and sometimes you do have to hit bottom before you can come back up—you recognize that to get back into balance, you need to start adding positive things into your life. For everyone, it's something different.

"Start off with music!

"If you're in a negative state and hearing about shooting or killing people or miserable relationships, drugs, or alcohol, try switching to something more positive. I always switch to reggae because it typically has such a positive vibe and a positive message. Then you also have to switch that self-talk to something more positive.

"Stop saying these things like 'I'm no good' or 'I'm a piece of shit' or 'I'll never succeed.' All of these negative words need to be consciously switched.

"Say it! Say, 'I'm good at this' and 'I can do this' and 'I am grateful for what I have!' That works to add more light to the darkness. These are just positive affirmations you can allow yourself to hear. We keep adding in those pieces—and this is part of the reason that we added this book into it all as well.

We put in the positivity in order to pick ourselves back up."

Erik approached the concept of equilibrium in your life in terms of working hard and playing hard: "If you're going to do these radical and ambitious things, you need to have the same radical and ambitious energy about your recovery and rest. That balance is so necessary."

Kyle sees equilibrium as commitment. "If I'm going to add to my craft or do something to provide value, I also need to live hard and enjoy things. Enjoy food, meet people, and do those things to the best of your ability just as hard as you are working. You need to have that joy in that life. It's something that's so out of balance.

"You don't have to go far to find someone who isn't overworked. Experiencing joy is being balanced! That feeling of fear—fear of loss or not having enough—that fear generates the idea that you have to work yourself to the bone and you don't deserve rest. When you are constantly saying you need to be better or need to make more money, much of it is driven from a fear of losing something.

"You counteract that with faith. Faith that it's going to be okay.

"If I want to go have dinner once a week with a friend of mine, and we're not working and not talking about work, that's okay! It's going to be fine! Everything is going to work out. If I take my wife out for dinner or for a nice treat even though things may be a little tighter, it's okay, because we'll figure it out. That's having faith in yourself that you will be okay, and you will adapt.

"Erik and I both got stuck in our old ways and our old jobs and our old methods because we were scared of what would happen if we let go and embraced Budo Brothers fully. We were scared the economy would crash or scared about the impact of Covid.

"But then we recognized that we are both really good at this. We are both able to adapt. So we had faith in ourselves and in each other that we could work this out. That's the balance. Take time to live in the moment and don't be scared about running out of money or time, because while you're frozen and scared of those things—working yourself to the bone—you're increasing the chance it's going to happen, or it's just going to happen anyway!"

Something was becoming very clear during our discussions about equilibrium. It takes trust. What Kyle was describing was trust both in himself and in Erik. Erik reciprocates that trust in Kyle. That's why Budo Brothers has worked as well as it has and seen great success. Balance is intrinsically linked to joy, but it also requires a level of trust in others and in yourself.

I asked Erik to expand on this idea. Here's what he added regarding trust: "Trusting yourself only comes from actually challenging yourself and your ideas. You have to realize that you've done things before, and you can do it again. You know you've been through rough times enough that you have faith in your own abilities. You are consistently working on yourself every fucking day. You work on yourself. That brings about the confidence in your ability to overcome challenges through trying new things.

"When life gets stale and boring, it's because you aren't challenging yourself. You aren't getting that sense of adventure and discovery you had as a kid. You aren't just going out and building the treehouse! You aren't fucking around and finding out!"

Kyle jumped in to finish off thoughts on equilibrium: "Life is simple. It's one of the most simple concepts you can observe. You look at nature and see it. The job of most things is to grow. Trees grow. Dogs grow. That's our job. We grow. Simple isn't easy, though. Simplicity can be difficult. So we throw in all of these mental scenarios—we think we need all of these things outside of ourselves that we don't need in order to make us feel like we're worthy.

"All of those things aren't outside of us, though. They're inside.

"We don't have balance because everything in the artificial physical world pulls us away from what is within. If you don't have faith in yourself and that you'll make the right choices, you need faith in something higher up. You are here to grow, yes, but you are also here to learn and experience things. The responses we have to those things aren't always going to be positive because they are all lessons. It's our responses to the lessons that are being delivered that's critical.

"The saddest thing I see is people being scared to grow, so they stay safe. They don't do anything. They've made it into an environment where they're comfortable, and they just stay where it's safe. They don't expand because they don't have equilibrium—they just start to atrophy. Smile! Love life! Dance! People are scared to dance in front of other people! Why are you scared to smile at someone! Why be scared to enjoy something? Why do you feel like you don't deserve the nice things in life?

"Listen, if someone gave me a billion dollars tomorrow, I'd be doing the exact thing I'm doing today because I enjoy it. I'd just be doing it louder! It's such a serious thing, and I feel it a lot too. It's that whole lack of money and being able to provide. It keeps so many people down, and it seems present in everyone's life. Having enough money to provide—to have gas and food. It's a societal trap, but we need to relax and inject joy into it all so we can defuse those negative feelings."

Erik wrapped up our thoughts on equilibrium like this: "When something is in equilibrium, the opposing forces are equal. So if you're too joyful and ecstatic, you aren't in a state of equilibrium. You need to be balanced. You've brought about balance where your insecurities are tempered by the confidence you have that you can do things. They're still there! But you have a state of balance.

"And when you've reached balance, you've reached a state of flow. That's when you're crushing it and you feel good. Perfect flow is hard because it takes equilibrium, and that's rare.

"Trust yourself. Maintaining equilibrium will require constant micro-adjustments. To balance a stick on my finger, I have to constantly micro-adjust. I maintain balance by tiny little movements that help me keep a stick balanced. If I start going too far, the stick falls down. But I know that I've done it enough times that it's easy to reach a state of balance.

"Once you stop making little adjustments, you are out of balance!"

Your Journey Through the Dark— Problem-Solving with Imagination

We have gained stability on our journey out of the darkened forest. We have lit our way, and we have balanced our progress to ensure that we are taking steps forward and leading ourselves into the clear.

Our next task is to not only handle the obstacles on our path but to feel confident and free solving those troubles with our own imagination.

That's creativity.

As we walk, we may briefly lose our way once more. We know, however, that we are able to persevere. We know our way, and we have the experience to keep ourselves on the right path. When problems arise, we create solutions.

If the torch begins to fade, we collect dry kindling and light one anew. If we lose our way, we retrace our steps and get back on the right path. Our creativity—letting us be ourselves and finding the solutions to the problems that persist—is the very nature of being human. That ability to create is what saves us from ending up right where we began.

We know now. We know how to lead ourselves out of the dark, and we do so confidently and creatively.

The clearing is just ahead. Let's keep walking.

Finding Your Creative Energy

Creativity is an expansive topic. Throughout history, man has harnessed creativity to create some of the great works of our time. Leonardo da Vinci's *Mona Lisa*, *The Thinker* by Rodin, the Sistine Chapel of Michelangelo, *The Starry Night* by Vincent Van Gogh, and the Great Pyramid of Giza are all breathtaking works of creativity and inspiration.

Maybe you could throw *Bill & Ted's Excellent Adventure* in there, too.

The point is, throughout human history, creativity is weaved into the fabric of who we are as a species. Other creatures do not paint or yearn to create a work showcasing the beauty—or darkness—of our shared humanity. We develop new tools and techniques to create stunning works of creative genius, and it is something that is a call within the very fabric of our souls.

And creativity is not just visual. Think of music! From Beethoven's "Moonlight Sonata" (easily the most beautiful piece of music my ears have ever enjoyed) to the first few chords of "Smells Like Teen Spirit," our hearts are enamored with emotion and song. Who hasn't thrown on a sad song to go with a sad mood or an uplifting tune to celebrate a great day? Each one of those artists had feelings of their own on the days they created that work, and through shared resonance, we speak to each other through creativity. The artist to us, and us to others.

All of this begs a question.

Where does it come from? And why does creativity matter?

It is true that many historical artistic works were tributes to God. Ancient marble sculptures, temples, and songs were created and understood as a higher power speaking through us. They were breathtaking and magnificent in every way, acting as this strange conduit through which something greater than us forged a path from a fleeting thought in a daydream to a work that stands through generations.

Like Pink Floyd's *The Wall* being discovered for the first time by high school potheads year after year, this creative energy—harnessed so long ago—hits on something so deep within each of us that it's impossible to classify it as a mere "hobby" or just something humans do when they're bored.

Being creative is wired into you, though you may not realize it. You may have a difficult time speaking to that part of yourself, or you may think you aren't creative at all. It is within each of us, but not all of us have figured out how to wire our frequency to hear that creative calling. We are, however, all artists in some way.

It's with this spirit in mind that I asked my friends the most straightforward question.

"What is creativity?"

Erik wanted to tackle this huge question: "To me, it's rooted in imagination. To imagine is the first seed of creating something that hasn't existed. You dream first. One thing we can all relate to is remembering when we were kids and having this inner child where you were playing with your friends, your imagination was running wild, and you were inside of that world. Cardboard was a real sword! Boxes were real castles!

"This imagination that we have as children gets beat out of us as we grow up.

"It's why kids are so imaginative. They're tapped directly into that part of themselves, and they aren't afraid of it. It allows them to say the craziest, funniest things. There's an innocence to it, and it gets worn out and worn down eventually.

"For me, the seed of creativity is imagination. I would sit there and think, 'I wonder if . . .' and some of the most incredible things come after those three little words. That's what happened with our Hood-Gi! I wonder if I took a hoodie and a gi, and I shoved it together? I imagined it in my head. Then I sketched it. Then I got someone to make a prototype, then I wore it, then people commented on it, then it snowballed!"

When we express creativity, we are expressing something new. It is something groundbreaking to us in our world. Those ideas reach out on the inside and grab us. They take hold, and they don't let go. Sometimes, we obsess to an unhealthy degree over our own creativity. Many artists have been driven mad—consumed by the creative inspiration that overwhelmed them. It's understanding that creative energy, letting go, and letting it work through you that's the trick to harnessing your own creativity.

And it is one of the healthiest things for your mind, body, and soul.

Kyle approached the topic of creative energy like this: "It's your full force. It's what elicits your creative muscle. Initially, I thought I wasn't creative. I'm terrible at art. I have bricks for hands. I hated making things in art class. I grew up thinking I wasn't creative or artistic at all.

"Self-expression has so many levels, though. It's yours. You can see it in the things your brain locks onto and comes up with creative solutions and pathways for. There are moments in our lives where our brains get lost in all of the different paths that our creativity establishes.

"To me, that's where creativity is birthed. It's when you get lost in your work or your passion. Time doesn't exist when you're lost in it; it's irrelevant. You're imagining and creating in this realm and space where you are just imagining everything, and the energy comes from doing it in a space where you are interested.

"It's hard to create things you don't care about. In those terms, it is somewhat out of your control but also somewhat within your control."

As an author, it's that creative state that is a constant, nearly everyday battle. Some days, all of the conditions for my success are set. I had a great breakfast, a nice cup of coffee, and I have nothing to do for the day except get the words down.

But the words don't want to get down.

Other days, I wake up like a bolt of lightning hit my ass at two a.m. because in a half-dreaming state I gathered an idea for a story that I'm working on that demands to be put to a notepad. It can be both exhilarating and frustrating all at once. I've long since accepted that creatively I work much like a roulette wheel. Some days, it's red when I've bet on red. Some days, it's black when I've bet on black. Some days, I luck out and hit the exact number I was thinking about, and my creative energy explodes with the force of an exploding star.

Each day, however, is vastly different than the next. No matter how hard I work toward creating the perfect conditions for creativity to flow, there is no guarantee that it will do so.

So I followed up the question on general creativity with something more specific. "Can you force yourself to be creative?"

Erik answered, "You can't tell someone to create a masterpiece with a deadline. It's too difficult. You need to know what ingredients optimize your own creativity. Whether you like it or not, you're always creating, and it's not necessarily art.

"You could be creating a super shitty life right now. And that's your own creation. You're responsible for it. It's based on the decisions you've made. We are, by definition of being alive, creating every single day. So what do we choose to create? What am I choosing to create today?

"Your life is art, and you are the artist! What are you choosing to manifest or create on a daily basis minute by minute and second by second?

"The important thing is to be ready to receive that creative idea. If you have to write it down in the middle of the night, do it. If you have to bounce ideas off of other people, do that. Whatever it is and however it strikes, embrace being the conduit. You have to be comfortable sitting in silence. You have to be comfortable being the listener to yourself. Be a blank slate, but start the process and be comfortable with not knowing what the end result is going to be. Play with your ideas!"

Kyle talked about creativity in terms of removing things from your life. "I think that for me, the creative process is less about adding things and more about removing. You know the energies and things that will make you not able to be creative. Stress, sickness, frustrations—that lightning rod of creativity is nowhere to be seen because of everything in the way. So you need to remove those stresses. Remove the outside noise so when creativity strikes, you can harness it. Good vibes!

"Some of our best ideas happen when we're on vacation. The vibes are good, the stresses are gone, the task list is smaller, and we have the space to be creative."

Erik added, "If you're really struggling with being creative, try something new. Be open. Be willing to do a new thing just to create for the sake of creating something. It doesn't have to be beautiful or perfect, and it doesn't have to have an end goal. Flex the creative muscle by creating for the sake of it! Play! Playing is where creativity happens! Play has no objective. Playing is the objective! It sets your mind free to imagine, and imagination leads to creativity!"

There is an endless well of creativity within you, and that creativity can unleash the most magnificent things in your life if you allow it to.

Relax. Listen to yourself. Start creating.

Once you do that, it's time to let your mind run wild and free!

Free Your Mind and Manifest

When our imagination is rolling full steam ahead, and creativity starts to show up, it can very much act like a pressurized hose is suddenly let loose. It sprays everywhere and in every direction. Sometimes it's hilarious. Sometimes you get soaked with ideas. Sometimes you have a hard time controlling the direction you need to divert it.

That state of creativity, however, is a state of imagination and joy. The troubles shrink, the worries lessen, and you can be fully absorbed into something wonderful in your own mind.

Creativity is inherently a joyous state of mind!

Erik explains, "Letting your mind run free is sitting with your thoughts. You let the waterfall of contemplation and ideas come and go through you. You explore all of the ideas and go into the uncharted waters to see what you can uncover. It requires freedom and detachment as well as openness to possibilities you never knew existed.

"When we were in Vietnam, it was one of our most creative spaces. We let the experience take over, and it put us into the zone. We were just playing, creating, and enjoying every moment of the process. We had no intention behind anything. We had no idea where we were going. We had no idea we'd be there, zero expectations. It's an iconic moment for us where we were able to be creative, and it was awesome!"

The genesis of Joy-Jitsu is a perfect example of creativity running wild and free. I received a phone call out of the blue, and it wasn't much more than Kyle saying, "Hey. We want to write a book, and we want you to do it with us!"

Fast-forward a few weeks, and the three of us were running around the woods at the foot of the Canadian Rockies, having incredible meals cooked on a campfire and not worrying about anything other than exploring all of the concepts and ideas that make Joy-Jitsu what it is. It was a perfect, free moment where our collective imagination ran wild and free—and played off of one another to enhance, challenge, and generate even more than we thought possible as individuals.

Kyle jumped on that idea: "This book didn't start as an idea for a book. We always wanted to get into something related to mindset. We wanted to help others think differently. But it was so organic that we didn't really think of it as a book. So we started the podcast, which you helped us launch, and that was another step on the creative journey. We wanted to fill in some blanks for people where we thought something was missing.

"It came out of a need. We were in the depths of Covid. It was a little seed that kept growing and we kept watering. We knew something was there that was fundamentally important. We're playing right now! We have no idea what the blossoms on this tree are going to look like.

"In my life right now, in terms of Joy-Jitsu, this has allowed me to play more than I ever have, and it's incredible."

A through line to all of these stories and all of these personal anecdotes is the fact that all of us manifest things that once only existed as synapses in our brains. Remember, as a human, you are designed to create. It brings a state of reflection, a state of joy, and a state of freedom that nobody and nothing can take from you.

A small idea turned into a business in Budo Brothers. Those ideas spawned even more ideas, some of which turned into a podcast. That podcast turned into more ideas, which became a foundation for Joy-Jitsu. After a few years, there's now a warehouse full of products, customers across the world, and millions of subscribers looking toward a specific type of content and message.

You are holding *Joy-Jitsu* because an idea happened, it was harnessed, and it has manifested into a book resting in your hands.

As Erik explains: "Creativity brings about things that don't exist. As humans, it separates us from the animals. We think and create, and we ask, 'What if?' We solve problems, and that elicits creativity. We don't have the answer to a problem—like product development—and we are constantly scanning our environment looking for the word *but*.

"You may hear someone say 'I like this, but...' Something is missing. The *but* is the unmet need. That's how we create and solve problems through our creativity. As entrepreneurs, we create abundance through solving other people's problems with creativity."

Kyle takes this way back into history: "A long time ago, fire was a creation. It was imagination that had us creating fires and using them to solve problems. These days we just use a lighter. You don't have to start over learning how to make a fire when you're born. Those ideas and challenges have already existed, and creation has already happened.

"The creations that came before from everyone have manifested already. You can now build on it and further it all! You leave things behind for the people after you. We continue to do that once our time is gone, and that's where your creations become your legacy and what you leave behind. These microcreations compound to make up the fabric of civilization. That's why we have the internet and incredible airplanes. The things we are doing today will absolutely inspire the next generation to do even more than we dreamed possible.

"You were put here to grow and to create. That's what you do, and that's what you leave behind. You leave behind children, language, and legacy. You cannot say you are not creative. You create every single day."

Erik expanded this even further: "It's Godlike! We were created in the image of God! Like, that's some divine shit that we are able to create things just as God has!"

There is no such thing as a human incapable of creating, and there is no state in which creativity cannot bring about an overwhelming feeling of joy.

Now it's up to you. Let your mind run wild and free, create, and manifest those ideas into the physical world!

Creativity as Therapy

Creating something requires a certain state of mind. Through creativity, we speak to ourselves, through ourselves, and to others. Creating allows us to express ourselves and our deepest imagination and thoughts into some kind of artistic medium. It may be painting, it may be writing, it may be song or dance. The act of creating is something humans do with purpose to self-express, and self-expression is healthy and necessary.

It is who we are.

I asked Erik about creativity as therapy to see what his take was. Here's what he had to say: "It feels good to create. It's calming and grounding. The process makes you converge on the moment and be present. It's therepeutic. Especially creating for the sake of creating and letting your imagination run wild. It is this process that brings about a state of peace and joy. By its very nature, just creating is therapeutic in so many ways.

"If you can, find things in your life you enjoy doing where there is no agenda, no end goal. You do it because you love it, not for money or fame. Raise animals, make pottery, paint, make music. All of these things are things humans do out of love. When you say, 'I love to,' whatever you say afterward is that creation waiting to happen, and that's your peace. Whenever you are down in the dumps or you are suffering, going into a therapy session of creating is highly effective to break that mood."

Kyle added: "If you look at a dog—its nature is to run around, chew on bones, and play in the grass. Our nature is to grow and create. When you are doing what you were put here on this planet to do, you feel good about it—that's therapy. When you're in a creative state, it's so soothing because you feel good about creating in that moment.

"In the moment, you are free! How many people just seek freedom? You get to live in these moments of free creation, and that in and of itself is therapeutic. You experience freedom through creativity."

I'm glad Kyle hit on criticism and what that can do.

One of the greatest roadblocks for any author is the notion of having your work criticized. It's a double-edged sword, for sure. Authors want to write and want their work in front of others, but we want to be shielded from the criticism that can naturally come with that.

Not everyone will love everything you do. That's a simple fact of having different people, personalities, and tastes upon this world. Some will resonate with your creative work, and some will not. I have had some incredible fans of my first published novel—some of them writing to me from across the world to tell me how much my work has meant to them in their life. I have also received criticism and bad reviews.

Long ago, I made a decision to treat my work as mine up until the moment I share it with others. At that point, it belongs to the reader, and I am free. My interpretation of my own work only matters to those interested in hearing alternate perspectives, but those words mean something to the person reading and how it resonates with them. In that way, we can let go of the fear of criticism.

It doesn't belong to you anymore once it is out there; it belongs to the reader, and each reader is different. That's how authors approach their work in a healthy way.

Kyle continued: "Once you put it out there, you are done with your creative process. You can reiterate and bring it back into your sphere and create more with it. Your creative process, though? When I'm creating videos, my creative process is over as soon as I publish it. Creativity? That happens when you're doing the filming, editing, the fancy cuts, and the music track. When you share it to the world, it's no longer creation. It's just waiting to be judged. We always talk about how it belongs to the internet after we create it. We do what we love, it meets all of our standards, we are happy with our work, and now it belongs to people.

"They can criticize it, love it, or be indifferent.

"That's what you do with art and a creative work. You put it out into the world. People will feel how they feel about it, but that is ultimately outside of your control. Creating it was within your control. Sometimes the majority dislike it. Sometimes the majority like it. Sometimes they don't care.

"I would much rather people love it or hate it than be apathetic. Indifferent means I didn't strike a chord with anyone. For all the people who dislike it, you know you struck a chord with those that love it.

"Look at Erik! He loves creating things! He loves to create and tinker and change and adjust because of how much he loves the creation process. He knows once it's out there, the process is over, and he hates that about it because he's so happy when he's creating!"

Erik jumped in. "It's so true! When I first moved into my condo, I needed some art on my wall. So I went to a store and was about to pick up this nice piece of abstract art. Then I thought to myself, 'I can do this!' I put the painting down, went to the craft store, dropped a few hundred bucks on paint and supplies, and started imagining what 'my artwork' would look like. Here's the crazy part, though. In my mind, I could see exactly what it looked like. The painting only existed in my consciousness. I locked myself in a room, and the paint strokes started to flow. I couldn't believe it! I was a conduit that birthed this creation! It didn't exist before, and now it does.

"It was at that point that I realized I can create anything I imagine. Anything I can think of, I can bring into the physical world. Now, that's exactly what I do with every single one of Budo Brothers' products. Each product begins with imagination. 'What would a Budo Brothers throwing knife look like?' Images start arriving in my mind, sketches start flowing, and before you know it, the CNC machine is coming to life, and prototypes are being born! This is the process I love. This is where time doesn't exist for me. This is where I feel powerful!"

I truly feel like these are some of the best pieces of advice for anyone in a creative field, whether their art is writing, drawing, crafts, or music. It's one of the biggest hang-ups for artistic types, being afraid of being criticized—by others or by yourself.

And this advice is for you, reading this book. Whatever it is that you enjoy creating, do so without fear and by honoring your own process and the joy you get out of it. Don't let the fear of some stranger's opinion hold you back in your life from enjoying the things you love the most. Don't let someone's cranky unsolicited opinion of you wreck your week, your day, or your mood in the moment. You create for you, and you are built as a human being to do it. So do it. Love every second of creation. By all means, if you wish to share your work to the world, do so and be prepared to ignore any and all feedback.

You've created. You have harnessed the joy of one of the most fundamental human traits. Be at peace with it, love the process, and never stop creating!

Provide Value Through Creativity

Not everything you do has to be monetized. Not everything you create needs to be in front of other people's eyes. We can create for ourselves and for our own joy. But what happens when your creation provides value?

Does every creation provide value?

Now, if we take an extreme example of a banana being taped to a wall as a form of "art," we can easily criticize it. Is fruit mounted on a wall with a strip of adhesive a work of art?

To my eyes? No. The banana belongs in my morning smoothie, and the duct tape can be used to hold together the handle on my broken, well-used lawnmower. To someone else, a banana taped to a wall may very well signify something dramatic. Fruit and adhesive becomes a metaphor for the struggle between man and his inner self, awaiting his eventual decay, held up as an example to all that pass of the true nature of his helpless nihilism.

You do you. I still think it's weird.

However, to someone, there is deep meaning within that work, and it speaks to them. In that way, it has created value in spite of the blatant absurdity of it. That work has an audience, and that audience may very well be moved deeply by what it represents.

That's the nature of creating and resonance. We create because it is within us to do so, and it brings us joy. We share it with others in the hope it will resonate and help them somehow. Kyle, Erik, and I are putting this book together for you because creating it has brought us joy, and it is within our nature to create. We are hoping to place it in your hands so that it may resonate and help you in your life.

That is the value we wish to create.

Erik explains: "Creativity is a process, so you create something and then find people that the creation is valuable to. So if your expression produces a work of art, the next challenge is finding the people who find value in your expression.

"Does a song you made calm them after a rough day of work? Does your painting stop people in their tracks because of its beauty? Does it give off a feeling of awe and wonder? Does your invention solve someone's awful problem?

"This is where we find the people we can serve through our own creation. That's what entrepreneurship is! You find your tribe!"

Kyle used me as an example: "David, you create stories that you know some people may not like, but you aren't creating it for them. You are literally doing this with projects you are working on! But you've made the decision of it being for a certain group of people, knowing another group may not like it. That's your creation providing value for a section of people. You created it because you wanted to write a great story, and you know you'll have an audience it resonates with.

"One of the best feelings in the world is designing an experience and creating something with intent. Erik does it all the time—he'll think of something, but he'll think of what that person will feel when they encounter that thing. You plan it out, but you don't know how the world receives it. He wants to elicit a feeling when someone opens a package from us with our gear in it. When you plan it out, and it gets received that way, it's such a good feeling! I'm sure that a person who writes a love song and hears about someone dedicating it to their partner gets that amazing feeling that they were able to foster such an emotional reaction.

"Take it to child bearing, even! If you create good humans and are a good parent, you create humans that are better for our society. Even being a mentor to someone else, whether it's coaching or helping someone's business, you are creating a better world."

Erik jumped back in: "Providing value through creativity is you being an entrepreneur. You are endeavoring to serve other people through what you see as valuable. You created something that has value to someone else. The more people you are able to then go and serve and improve, the more your life improves as a result! The more people you help, the more problems you solve, the more abundant your life will be."

At this point, Erik asked me to define the word *service*.

We'll call it "the action of helping or doing work for someone."

Erik jumped on it: "You are assisting and improving someone else's life. You are serving. Just opening a door for someone is being of service to others. This whole piece of creativity and using creativity to be of service to others is a beautiful thing.

"You are taking something that doesn't exist. You manifest it. Now, you're the one that can give that creation life by allowing it to improve other people's lives. Being of service to others through creativity is a great feeling. You feel good when you are valued. When you can bring about valuable solutions and aspects to people's lives, by definition you are a valuable human with something valuable to say. You are serving other people through your own imagination and creativity!

"If it's an idea for a product of some kind, it's incredible! You noticed a problem that needed to be solved. You imagined a solution. You created and manifested that solution, and now you have people paying you for it! That process is going to give you more fuel to create more and to be of service to more people. You continue to grow, provide more value, and you get to create even more and give other people that value!"

Kyle wanted to wrap up the thoughts on creativity: "One of the most mind-blowing things about value to me is the stock market. Someone is finding something valuable at the same exact point where someone is finding it not valuable. One person is selling; one person is buying. It blows my mind, but it speaks to how different people see value in different things and in different ways. In stocks, you are buying something someone else is just selling! How wild is that! Some people find value in collectibles. People have Pogs, stamps, Beanie Babies, or baseball cards.

"One thing that's common, though, is helping people solve problems. That's always valuable, and everyone will find that valuable. In order to solve a problem, you create a solution. Finding a bare wall in your house is a problem, so you go for a solution and find someone's artwork to hang up. There's a need and a solution. It's like a weird chicken and egg thing—you want to feel valuable and needed, so you do that by solving someone else's problem or solving your own problem and sharing it with others!"

Your problem may not require tape and a piece of fruit, but whatever it is that you are working through with creativity, it is guaranteed that there is some need for it. Out there, you have a tribe of people that will appreciate your art, your music, your invention, or your thoughts.

Create, my friends. And create with an eye toward service. In our next section, we will talk all about being of service to others. Let's continue our path of Joy-Jitsu!

Your Journey Through the Dark— The Helping Hand

And here we are.

At one time, we were lost in the dark, cold and confused. We persevered and accepted our circumstance.

Then we were lost with nothing more than a match flame and a yearning to be better. Gratitude helped us feel safe and ready.

Our authenticity shone like a raging campfire, and we became confident that we would find our way out.

Our purpose led us on the path.

Our growth allowed us to gain more confidence with every step.

Balance allowed us to keep moving forward while reserving our strength for the journey ahead.

Creativity let us solve the problems along the way.

Now, service.

As we walk free of the woods, we are greeted with loved ones, friends, and strangers alike. Many of these people will end up in that dark forest, and they will not know the way out. They will be alone and suffering, as we once were.

But we have walked that path. While you can't tell someone not to be depressed or to simply be happier, you can prepare them and support them in the simplest way. You can hand them the match, just as someone handed it to you. You can offer a hand up to help them persevere. Let them light their own way and find their own path using all the principles of Joy-Jitsu that you've just experienced. You can be of service in the best way possible.

Be a sensei.

Be the one who has come before.

Let's get started.

Help Others to Help Yourself

If you take away anything from the following sections, let it be these words:

"It is not about you."

People often think of "service" in the same way they think of "charity," and not in a good way. It's seen as giving up a lot for little return. Offering your time, energy, and effort to something that is purely for others and that offers little to no personal gain (which is the point of it being "charity," but don't get me started there).

What is often not realized is the immense benefit service to others provides for you as an individual. Imagine where we would be as people, or as a society, if sharing knowledge and information was either forbidden or somehow seen as detrimental personally.

Have you ever looked up a video or article about how to solve an issue or accomplish something that you were unable to figure out?

I've rebuilt part of a home in part by looking up techniques for framing and drywall. I've learned guitar, podcasting, and how to self-publish books because of good people being in service to others and sharing their knowledge. I've had mentors in martial arts drive for hours to come and be a part of my dojo to help train students and support my efforts in running a school, and I reciprocated to add value to their school and their students.

This exchange of experience is more than just charity. This is what we do as humans in a society based on connections. We work together, pull together, share information. We better ourselves along with helping others do the same.

I learned more about myself, my skills, and my abilities when I devoted a great deal of time and focus to being a mentor for others—be it in martial arts or in writing. I became a better writer by helping writers, and I became a better martial artist by offering my experience and knowledge to other martial artists.

Erik puts this into perspective by explaining the simple purpose of an everyday household object: the extension cord.

"We can short-circuit ourselves if we are only focusing on me, me, me. It is literally like taking an extension cord and plugging it into itself. You can't expect anything to light up. The only way you can have that cord be useful is if it's actually plugged into an external socket. The trap of 'me, myself, and I' is a bitch to get out of. Especially if you start thinking with a scarcity mindset.

"If you come from a place of lacking things, you start thinking, 'If they get this, there's nothing for me,' so you fall into this hoarding mode where you don't want to share anything. That's a one-way road that doesn't lead to fulfillment or satisfaction or contentment. It just leads to misery. It leads to fixating on your own issues so much that you just create your own problems."

You can also think of this as a black hole. I'm a nerd for anything related to the cosmos—it is infinite and fascinating, and some of the most fascinating objects are black holes.

Black holes consume everything around them. They eat planets, they eat stars, they eat all matter, and light itself cannot escape them. The more they devour what is around them, the larger and hungrier they are for more. This all goes to a point called *singularity*. So massive and powerful is their hunger that there is a point close to the black hole where escape is impossible, and this is where information dies.

Being consumed by a black hole means (in theory, of course—let's not get into quantum mechanics) that there is a point where existence is over. There is no record of an object existing, it is impossible to see evidence of it, and it is simply gone.

This happens to us as humans when we get so wrapped up in keeping things to ourselves. The thoughts and experiences that we could use to help others end up swallowed up by our own ego and, over time, lost. Our own memory fades, and our own clarity suffers. It is our own psychological version of a singularity. There is a point when we keep consuming and hoarding that the information we held at our fingertips at one time has in all ways disappeared. We could have used it to lift up others, and we could have used it to lift up ourselves, but through our own misplaced greed, that treasure of experience becomes a forgotten memory, as if it never existed at all.

What a waste.

Imagine the world if artists never shared their work? Art galleries missing the likes of Monet or van Gogh. Music missing the likes of Mozart, Louis Armstrong, or the Beatles. What would culture look like without true change-makers like Bob Marley or Miles Davis?

Yes, many of these artists reached untold heights of personal success and fame, but they also shared. They were driven to be in service to others through their God-given talent and voice.

That service changed the world.

Erik continued:

"When we say it's not about you, if you are in a funk of some kind, one of the best things you can do is to go help someone and do something for someone else. Volunteer. Offer help. Even just listening. Be an open friend! Be helpful and resourceful for others. By serving others, you feel good and they feel good. It's a symbiotic relationship that creates community, and if those bonds are strong, they can serve you for the remainder of your life."

I wanted to explore this thought, so as soon as Erik was finished answering, I posed this follow-up question: "What about people who say, 'I have to think about myself right now'? Do you think it's possible to be selfish and in service at the same time?"

Both Erik and Kyle jumped on that question.

Erik went first. "Listen, we have to put our own oxygen mask on first before assisting others. But if you've gotten to this point in *Joy-Jitsu*, you've already done that!"

Kyle followed. "Service is the ethos of Budo Brothers. Budo is the way of the warrior, and in the hardest of times, we rely on warriors.

"The warrior's job is to serve their community and protect. Without them, you can't have a civilization. This whole ecosystem we live in is because people have interconnected. Life isn't a solo experience. You have to interact. You have to have some kind of community with others. It's part of the human experience. If you keep a human isolated for a long period of time, crazy shit happens! It is a necessity for humans to interact with one another.

"When you make your overall goals bigger than yourself, it can make the harder times seem less hard.

"If you're to look at what's going on in the world, the best you can do is adding kindness and love and participation. It makes the big issues less serious.

When you zoom out, it makes your problems seem small in comparison to the grandiose nature of it all."

There is a reason one of the worst punishments a society can lay upon someone who has committed a crime is isolation—known as *solitary confinement.* Many of us experience this in society, and the psychological consequences of being disconnected from others has the potential to ripple through generations of humans.

Our nature and instinct as people is to share critical information in a selfless way. A village with one hunter who doesn't share hunting techniques with the rest of his tribe will surely face eventual starvation. A farmer growing crops who fails to offer help to a fellow farmer in need can expect the same grace when falling upon similar hard times.

One of my favorite service-related stories is about whiskey.

In 1996, a fire ripped through the Heaven Hill bourbon distillery in Bardstown, Kentucky. Bourbon is a cutthroat industry. Approximately 95 percent of the world's bourbon exists within a seventy-five-mile radius in the state of Kentucky. The competition is fierce, the major distilleries are all neighbors, and they are all fighting for profit and market share. When Heaven Hill lost ninety thousand barrels of flaming bourbon—a fire so intense that firefighters were unable to get closer than about three hundred yards from the inferno—they were crippled among their competitors.

What did those competitors do? Did they celebrate or further shut down competition by taking advantage of one family's misfortune?

No. They stepped up. Rival distilleries offered to help distill, house, and transport Heaven Hill's bourbon as they rebuilt. Their employees and those families still had jobs in the face of seven full warehouses of full barrels lost in an inferno bolstered by fifty-mile-per-hour winds. A fire that devastated 2 percent of the world's bourbon in one night—casting flames twenty stories into the sky—was beaten by a sense of community and service to others.

And what happened?

Four years later, it was the year 2000 and the bourbon industry saw its first upward trend in production and sales since 1970. Bourbon whiskey has had a renaissance, and through the pulling together of a community of rivals being in service to one another, bourbon today is a near ten-billion-dollar industry and Heaven Hill's offerings are one of the top-three-selling whiskeys in the world.

That's not charity. That's not ego. That's being in service to those in a time of need, and as a result, an entire industry has grown and seen immeasurable success.

That is the power of service.

Start with Fruit

Let's get a little abstract and talk about ecosystems.

In complex natural ecosystems, you have a biodiverse range of flora and fauna (that's plant and animal for those who aren't familiar with the terms). You have plant matter that decays and is eaten by bugs and fungi. That perfectly fresh, nutrient-rich soil is just right for trees to grow and fruit. Animals eat the fruit, seeds fall to the floor, new plant matter grows, and the cycle moves on.

Everything in an ecosystem plays an important part in order to keep everything in balance. What we really want to focus on is that fruit. Be it apple, pear, pomegranate, or coconut, that fruit has a lot to teach us about providing service.

Erik explains it this way:

"It's a beautiful way that the ecosystem works. Each node within the system—even though operating from a place of self-service—the act of that also serves another objective. The animal is hungry; the tree wants to spread seed. The beginning interaction between the objective of the tree to propagate and grow is to start with something sweet—fruit.

The fruit is the prize. We start with that. The animal doesn't go plant a seed and then get fruit. The animal eats the fruit, which results in seeds being spread."

(Author's note: To be clear, this is because animals are either messy eaters and discard seed everywhere, or they're pooping them out. If you have a garden, I hope you've planted your own fruits and veggies with a more efficient method. One that won't cause you to devour fruit like a savage in your front yard in the hopes of getting seeds everywhere, or worse, horrify your neighbors with the latter method.)

Erik continued, "The whole beginning of that process starts with the tree serving the animal. In return, there's a symbiosis. That's where we can take a page out of nature. Start providing value to others. Begin everything with value. Start with service. This allows you to reach your objective, but it's starting with value first."

Kyle put this into perspective in terms of our symbiosis in creating this *Joy-Jitsu* book you're holding:

"You could have easily told us, 'Okay, guys, I'm gonna come up there and help you write this book, but it's gonna cost you something per hour.' But you said, 'Okay, I'm going to start with service.' You are helping us, and this opportunity helps you. This all works out into a symbiotic relationship eventually.

If we didn't start with helping each other in mind, it would've been a much harder energy to work with."

Think of what happens when an ecosystem remains flourishing on its own. More animals are attracted. More fruit is consumed, more seed spreads, and more fruit becomes available. Trees offer that fruit as a way to propagate outward. More trees provide more cover, more critters are attracted to the ecosystem, and it moves forward.

Eventually, a full, flourishing root system grows, the soil is incredibly fertile, and more vegetation grows. Eventually, as trees grow old and the fruit drops, leaves drop, and there is decay, an entire ecosystem of insects and fungi devour what remains, turn the soil into more nutrient-rich land, and more grows as a result. This cycle is critical to understand when it comes to service.

Erik put it in perspective in terms of our favorite fuzzy buzzing friends, the honeybee. "Bees want to make honey. During that process, they leave the hive to gather pollen. They jump flower to flower, pollinate, more flowers grow. It forms the backbone of so many ecosystems. If the bees fail, it all falls down. Without pollinating insects, everything will collapse."

Kyle ran with that thought. "Think of society! In religion, you are in service to God. In the military, in service to your country. You are bigger than yourself in every way as part of something more. You connect to the world in this way."

Whether you chose to be a part of it or not, you are involved in multiple systems and complex ecosystems by simply existing in life. By being a consumer, you give the opportunity to others to create and provide. By gaining skills and helping others, you are able to gain more skills and opportunities. By taking advantage of those opportunities, you are able to do more and further your own goals.

Leveraging that ecosystem by starting with being of value is what can create abundance for you and everything you choose to be involved with.

Ecosystem and Evolution

In the prior section, we talked about starting with fruit in order to build and flourish in your own incredible ecosystem, but what happens when the balance is upset?

Erik described it this way: "If something in the ecosystem no longer plays a role which benefits the ecosystem in some way, there is no need for it. It goes extinct. Some animals no longer serve a purpose. And sometimes it's difficult to see. Why do wasps exist? No, seriously? They're nothing but a bunch of assholes. Why do we have to put up with their shit?

"But they're necessary! They take out the garbage! They are the recycle team, much like fungus. They clear the dead growth to make fertile soil for brand-new seeds to germinate. Every little thing has a place in the ecosystem and plays a role. If you don't have a role and don't have a vital service to whatever it is—and it might be small—but if there's no reason for you to exist, nature has a great way of being efficient and kicking you out.

"If you're part of a team or part of a board of directors at a company, and you are the one that only takes, you are extractive. You should not be there. You are the one that should be extinct on that board, because you are a drain on the ecosystem. You aren't pushing the cart or helping.

"You are an invasive species at that point, and you should be gone."

Kyle saw a parallel in terms of how Budo Brothers reaches out and finds an audience: "Look at it in terms of our content! We make more income and have more reach by giving content away for free as opposed to charging for everything behind some kind of paywall. It's more in line with serving our customers. The ecosystem works itself out! What we figured out is that our customers want videos, we put them out for free, which is valuable to Google because they'll advertise, and Google pays us for advertising. This is an ecosystem that feels good and works for everybody."

I was curious to dive into this topic. How does someone who is a lone person start a process like starting with service. What if your ecosystem doesn't yet exist?

What is the first step in leading a service-driven life?

On this topic, Kyle recommended caution. "A lot of people are only focused on what they can get in return, and that's a trap. Your motivation matters. When you're in service, you give without expectation in return, which is incredibly difficult. It takes a lot of practice. Even when we started doing that, initially it took us time to get our heads around that, and we're certainly not perfect at it.

"Service means, 'I'm going to do something, and I don't care if it comes back.' That's such a hard thing to teach! Maybe Erik can clarify?"

Erik jumped in: "You need faith! Faith is critical. Part of service is trusting that there are forces at play that you don't have control over. For every action, there is an equal and opposite reaction. Call it karma or luck or whatever. The basis around it is simple.

"If you do shitty things, you create shitty results.

"If you do good things, good things are returned.

"If you serve people, you are better off. You make them better, and that makes you better and other people better. You are pollinating."

Kyle agreed. "And you need some faith in humanity! If you don't have faith that there is good out there, you won't want to give anything. If you think the world is going to end, you're holding all of your cards to yourself. If you have faith that we're going to be fine as a civilization, you'll want to serve the community and be a participant. And truly, faith in some kind of higher power as well. Everybody needs to have some type of faith in something—yourself, God, Allah, the universe, nature—something that is a force bigger than you. There are so many things that are too complex for our simple brains."

This is one of my favorite topics to explore. We have all kinds of systems that have been in place for all time. The evidence is right in front of you. Systems have been in place grinding away for millennia, and it's not going to stop.

Erik jumped on that thought. "And you know what? Every time man tries to fuck with it, he gets corrected. Play stupid games, win stupid prizes."

Kyle agreed. "Giving without expectation is really key. That's what you have to understand so you don't just think you'll wither away giving everything and receiving nothing in return. You don't want to always end up disappointed, and that's what happens if you give with expectations. If I offer you a gift with an expectation that you'll be super excited, and you aren't as excited as I envisioned, all of a sudden I feel disappointment. I set myself up for it.

"If instead I have no expectations, and I'm satisfied that I created something amazing and am happy that I thought of you and have zero expectations as to how that gift will be received, then it doesn't matter.

"If you think you'll be of service in order to get rich, it's the wrong outlook. Because you give without expectation, you have to have faith that it will all work out. You need to know that if you give, you can have faith in the long run that it will work out. Faith is an incredibly important part of service."

When you are in service to others, and you have faith that you are doing the right thing, you are taking care of yourself. Being in service isn't a detriment to yourself. You are simply offering fruit with faith that seeds will be planted, germinate, and grow.

Enjoy the act of service, because that's where joy is yours for the taking!

Thank You

This book was an amazing journey, and we are so grateful for David helping us put it together. Through this process, we have gained a lifelong friend.

And thank you, dear reader.

I want you to know that we believe in you, and we love you. Erik and I are incredibly fortunate to have an outstanding support system in our families, loved ones, and the community we've created. We're often brought to tears at the realization of how blessed we are to have unconditional love and support. This support system has given us the courage to try, fail, and be bold in pursuing what we love. And because of this precious gift, we're committed to giving back and supporting others in the same way we've been supported.

As you know, the first step in this journey is perseverance. It's essential to know that you're not alone. And we believe in you! Joy, happiness, and fulfillment are never-ending pursuits. It's a challenging path, but you are a warrior. You're perfect just the way you are. You're now part of a community of warriors—the "Budo Brothers and Sisters"—who are on a mission to spread joy and make a difference in the world. We want to express our heartfelt gratitude to you for reading this book. It means everything to us. And we want you to know that we're here to support you every step of the way. You're capable of achieving greatness, and we're thrilled to see what the future holds for you.

Now, I'd like to leave you with one last thing. Take two deep breaths, smile, and exhale. Repeat after me: "It is a good life." Because it truly is. Life is full of challenges, but it's how we approach those challenges that matters most. With courage, perseverance, and the support of your fellow warriors, you can conquer anything.

So go out there and seize the day, my friend. Be the warrior you were born to be, and spread joy, happiness, and love wherever you go. Remember that you're never alone and that we're all in this together.

With love,
Erik & Kyle

BUDO BROTHERS
WWW.BUDOBROTHERS.COM

YouTube: www.youtube.com/budobrothers

Instagram: www.instagram.com/budobrothers/

Facebook: www.facebook.com/budobros/

TikTok: www.tiktok.com/@budobrothers

Twitter: www.twitter.com/budobrothers

DAVID BADURINA
WWW.DAVIDBADURINA.COM

Twitter: www.twitter.com/DavidBadurina

Rumble: www.rumble.com/dbadurina/

Instagram: www.instagram.com/dbadurina_author/

YouTube: www.youtube.com/davidbadurina